Basic Bible Sermons on Philippians

To Francis —
a dear + long-
time Lubbock +
New Mexico friend

JB. Fowler
1991

BASIC BIBLE SERMONS

ON

PHILIPPIANS

J. B. Fowler

BROADMAN PRESS
NASHVILLE, TENNESSEE

© Copyright 1991 • Broadman Press
All rights reserved
4222-77
ISBN: 0-8054-2277-3
Dewey Decimal Classification: 227.6
Subject Heading: BIBLE. N.T. PHILIPPIANS—SERMONS
Library of Congress Catalog Card Number: 00-00000
Printed in the United States of America

Unless otherwise stated, all Scripture quotations are from the Holy Bible, *New International Version,* copyright © 1973, 1978, 1984 by International Bible Society.

Scriptures marked KJV are from the *King James Version* of the Bible.

Library of Congress Cataloging-in-Publication Data

Fowler, J. B., 1930-
    Basic Bible sermons on Philippians / J. B. Fowler, Jr.
        p. c.m. — (Basic Bible sermons series)
    ISBN 0-8054-2277-3
    1. Bible. N.T. Philippians—Sermons. 2. Baptists—Sermons.
3. Sermons, American. I. Title. II. Series.
BS2705.4.F69 1991   91-10199
252'.061—dc20   CIP

To Wanda Orrick Fowler,
my wife for nearly forty years;
Beulah Orrick,
faithful Sunday School teacher in
First Baptist Church, San Antonio, Texas;
the late Cecil Orrick,
faithful deacon in First Baptist, San Antonio;
and John and Katherine Richardson,
San Antonio

Other Books in the Basic Bible Sermons Series:

Basic Bible Sermons on the Cross, W. A. Criswell
Basic Bible Sermons on Easter, Chevis F. Horne
Basic Bible Sermons on John, Herschel H. Hobbs
Basic Bible Sermons on the Church, Ralph Smith
Basic Bible Sermons on Hope, David Farmer
Basic Bible Sermons on Spiritual Living, Stephen B. McSwain

Contents

Foreword

I have known Dr. J. B. Fowler, Jr., since 1968. We were fellow pastors in Lubbock, Texas, for five years. We have been fellow staff members for the Baptist Convention of New Mexico since 1985, where Dr. Fowler has been editor of the *Baptist New Mexican* since 1981.

Dr. Fowler has a deep commitment to Bible preaching. Because he pastored for thirty years, he understands the help a pastor needs if he is to have two fresh, Bible-centered sermons every Sunday, and a Bible study that feeds the people at the Wednesday prayer meeting service.

These sermons on the Book of Philippians, often called the book of "Joy," will be a help to any pastor. The titles are appealing but not sensational. The outlines are straight from the text. In these pages you will find homiletics at its best. The illustrations are alive and give strong explanation to the passages of Scripture. The illustrations used in the conclusion of each sermon are worth the price of the book. What pastor has not longed for a fitting illustration to close a sermon? These closing illustrations are a fitting climax to each sermon.

Any pastor, Sunday School teacher, or student of the Scriptures will find the Book of Philippians a helpful message from the pen of the imprisoned, joy-filled apostle Paul. And the reader of Dr. Fowler's sermons will find a relevant message for daily living.

Claude Cone
Executive Director
Baptist Convention of New Mexico
Albuquerque, N.M.

1
Are You Majoring on Minors?

(Phil. 1:1-11)

Introduction

Some years ago I came across one of the saddest statements I ever read. The biographer of Horace Walpole, an eighteenth-century English author, wrote about Walpole: "All his tastes were minor."

Apparently the biographer meant that Walpole stumbled through life, never seeing—even in his dreams—the things most magnificent and most desirable.

"All his tastes were minor." What a sad epitaph.

When I read that sad commentary, I remembered another thing I had read about an unnamed man whose horizons must have been as low as Walpole's.

At six months of age this man could recite the alphabet. At two he could read. Before he was three he had invented a formula for remembering important historical dates. At eleven he entered Harvard University and graduated with straight A's. And at forty-eight he died in a rented room, barren except for the evidence of his favorite hobby: collecting streetcar transfers from all over the United States.

His biographer could have written of him, as was written of Walpole, "All his tastes were minor."

This text at which we are looking now addresses us, probes our hearts, and forces us to ask ourselves, "Am I majoring on minors?"

Paul, who had not seen his Philippian friends for some time, was concerned about their spiritual welfare. He had heard of their quarrelsome, divided spirit. He feared they had shelved things of monumental importance and were majoring on minors, so he wrote to encourage them to "approve things that are excellent" (v. 10, KJV). He told them to get out of life's minor key and major on things of major importance.

You and I must also be on guard against living in life's minor key. It is a subtle temptation that threatens each of us. To help guard against majoring on minors, Paul showed us two things to remember: our position in Christ and our privileges in Christ.

Our Great Position in Christ

John Dewey, an American university professor and philosopher, said: "The deepest urge in human nature is the desire to be important."

The people to whom Paul wrote held no lofty, worldly positions. They were Roman citizens, chiefly Greeks, who lived in a lonely outpost far from Rome. Most of them were poor. Yet, as humble followers of Jesus Christ, Paul told them that they held in Jesus Christ the greatest position possible. What he said of them is also true of us.

We Are Servants of Jesus Christ

According to the late Greek scholar Kenneth Wuest, there are five Greek words in the New Testament translated by the English words *servant* or *slave*. Two of these words are used in verse 1. The first is translated "servants" and the other is translated "deacons": "Paul and Timothy, servants of Christ Jesus, to all the saints of Christ Jesus at Philippi, together with the overseers and deacons."

Wuest wrote that "servants" translates the word *doulos*. The *doulos* was a slave or servant born into slavery. He or she was bound to a master in a relationship to be broken only by death. The *doulos* had no will of his own, but lived only to obey his/her master. The word was used in the first century to describe the most abject, servile condition.

Paul wrote that he and Timothy were "servants" of Christ Jesus. We are to understand that we, too, are Christ's servants.

We were born into that relationship. It's called the new birth, and Jesus talks about it in John 3.

As a servant, our will is to be subjected to the will of our Savior. He is the Master. We are His servants. We are to place His interests above our interests.

Although the *doulos* was the most abject slave of the household and lived in the most servile conditions, as Christ's servants our position is reversed: we are "a kingdom and priests" (Rev. 1:6; 5:10; also see 20:6). But we are to live before Christ in the kind of humble spirit that characterized a first-century household slave.

The other word for *servant* is translated "deacons." It is the word, *diakonos,* and comes from a verb which means "to pursue" or "to hasten after."

Diakonos, which shows the servant actively engaged in his work, is also translated by the words "minister," "servant" and "deacon." It appears then that *doulos* more describes the servant's condition, and *diakonos* more describes the servant's activity.

We Are Saints in Christ Jesus

Paul addressed the quarreling Philippians as "saints in Christ Jesus" (v. 1).

Every believer is a saint but all are not saintly! As we grow in grace, however, we move toward becoming "saintly saints." It is both positional and progressive.

The word means "holy ones." It is used in the New Testament to describe both things and people that have been set apart by God for Himself and for His service. The word is translated "saints" approximately sixty-three times in the New Testament. Everyone who has been saved is a saint. This is the word used most often in the New Testament to describe one who is trusting in Jesus.

In his booklet *Live Sermon Outlines,* Ian MacPherson wrote about a grocer in Edinburgh, Scotland, who was named James Saint.

A man who knew James Saint wrote a letter to him on one occasion but mistakenly addressed it to "James Saint, Aberdeen, Scotland."

When the letter reached Aberdeen, the postal people searched diligently, but could not find anyone in their town named James Saint. So they returned the letter to the sender with a notation on the envelope: "There are no Saints in Aberdeen. Try Edinburgh." MacPherson says this might be called "the case of the missing saint."

Look in your telephone directory. Are there any "Saints" in your town? According to the telephone people, you may not have a single saint in your town!

But that's according to the telephone company. According to the Lord Jesus, all who believe in Him are "saints in Christ Jesus" (v. 1).

We are servants. But more than that, we are saints!

Our Great Privileges in Christ

One day a woman was looking down from the Empire State Building in New York City. Seeing the ant-like people crawling along on the street far below, she exclaimed: "I guess that is the way people look to God."

Oh no! That isn't how God sees us and thinks of us. He sees us as infinitely important and precious and desires for us only "Grace and peace to you from God our Father and the Lord Jesus Christ" (v. 2). Infinitely loved by Him, and having grace and peace are only two of the believer's great privileges in Christ.

We are so precious to God that He has given us the greatest privileges in heaven or on earth available to mortals: that of being His sons and daughters, enjoying His grace and peace, and having fellowship with Him.

When the magnificent truth that we sons and daughters of men have the inestimable privilege of being sons and daughters of God breaks upon us in all its glory and joy, we will determine not to spend our days majoring on minors!

Look at the three great privileges noted in these verses that belong to every believer.

We Are the Recipients of Divine Grace

"Grace . . . to you," Paul exclaims in verse 2.

It is in the form of a prayer. Paul is praying for the Philippian believers, reminding them that they have received God's grace and praying that it shall continue to abound.

The word *grace* appears about 125 times in the New Testament. It is a choice word used more by Paul than by any other New Testament writer. No word in the New Testament is richer in meaning.

Before the word came into the Holy Scriptures, it was used by the Greeks to speak of a favor one friend did for another friend out of generosity, with no thought of being rewarded.

But when it came into the Scriptures, its meaning was lifted and ennobled.

God's grace that we have received, and do receive in Christ, points back to the cross where God "so loved [us] that he gave his only begotten Son" (John 3:16, KJV). There God did a favor for us that far surpasses all that anyone ever did for a friend. But God did it not for those who were friendly toward Him but for those in rebellion against Him. Paul states this very clearly in Romans: "When we were God's enemies, we were reconciled to him through the death of his Son" (5:10).

Those who really see, understand, and experience what God did for them at Calvary simply cannot spend their life majoring on minors!

But there is a second great privilege that is ours:

We Are the Recipients of Divine Peace

"And peace to you from God our Father and the Lord Jesus Christ" (v. 2).

Again, Paul's words are both a prayer and an encouragement. He was reminding the Philippians that they had received the peace of God through Christ and praying that God's peace would fill and flood their lives.

The New Testament speaks of peace with God (Rom. 5:1) and

the peace of God (Phil. 4:7). Peace with God comes when we are saved. The war is over. Peace has been made through the blood of Christ (Col. 1:20). We have accepted Christ and are no longer in rebellion against God. We have been reconciled to God through Christ Jesus (2 Cor. 5:18).

There is something more. This reconciliation should be followed by the peace of God that fills our hearts in all circumstances of life. But no one can have the peace of God until he or she has peace *with* God.

This peace of God in daily life, according to Paul, is "from God our Father and the Lord Jesus Christ" (v. 2). They have a monopoly on it. Only God can give peace to a troubled life, and He mediates this peace through Jesus Christ His Son (Acts 4:12).

Peace with God is God's grace gift to the unbeliever who repents and accepts Christ. The "peace of God" is God's grace gift to the believer for all of his or her needs in life.

In his Greek-English lexicon, Joseph Henry Thayer defined "peace," as Paul used it here, as: "The tranquil state of a soul assured of its salvation through Christ, and so fearing nothing from God and content with its earthly lot, of whatever sort that is." Thayer added that this is "a conception distinctly peculiar to Christianity."

Eric Barker was a missionary from Great Britain who served more than fifty years in Portugal.

During World War II, life in Portugal became so dangerous that Barker was advised to send his wife and eight children to England for safety. His sister and her three children were also evacuated on the same ship. Barker remained behind to conclude some missionary matters.

When he stood to preach the next Lord's Day morning, he told his congregation he had just received news that his family had safely arrived home.

It was not until later that the congregation understood what Barker had meant. They thought he meant his family was safe in England, but that wasn't the case.

Just before he went into the pulpit to preach that Sunday morning, he had been handed a telegram telling him that a German submarine had torpedoed the ship on which his family was sailing. All passengers had perished. They had arrived safely home, not to England, but to heaven where Jesus had welcomed them!

This peace, which it is our privilege to have, is divine rest in the midst of life's most difficult struggles. Like Barker, we can have peace in our hearts, regardless of what happens because our peace comes not from our circumstances but from our Lord. He is our peace.

There is here one final privilege that belongs to the Christian. Remembering it and taking it to heart will strengthen us against majoring on minors.

We Are the Recipients of a Divine Fellowship

In verses 3-8, Paul speaks of the blessed fellowship that he and the Philippians enjoyed in Christ: "I thank my God every time I remember you. In all my prayers for all of you, I always pray with joy because of your partnership in the gospel from the first day until now" (vv. 3-4).

Although he had not seen these friends for several years, Paul remembers them and still enjoys a warm fellowship with them. He writes here to express his gratitude to them for the fine manner in which they had stood by him through the years. In the words of our well-known hymn, Paul was saying:

> Blest be the tie that binds
> Our hearts in Christian love;
> The fellowship of kindred minds
> Is like to that above.

Paul's fellowship with the believers was sweet; and 2,000 years removed from Paul, it is still sweet. The sweetness of the Christian fellowship has not diminished one degree with the passing of centuries.

What a blessing it would be if every pastor, long years after his ministry has ended in a certain place, could remember the fellowship with those who were once his people, as Paul did, and say of them: "I thank my God every time I remember you" (v. 3).

But we can't always do that. Pastors and people alike, majoring on things of minor importance, leave too many black scars rather than bright stars on their memories.

Finally, in verses 9-10, Paul prayed that the Philippians would not waste themselves on minor matters: "And this is my prayer: that your love may abound more and more in knowledge and depth of insight, so that you may be able to discern what is best and may be pure and blameless until the day of Christ."

I like the way the *King James Version* sums up this important matter of majoring on things of major importance. "That ye may approve things that are excellent" (v. 10).

Paul tells them that the most excellent things in life are an overflowing love for the things of God, a sincere, dedication of themselves to God (v. 9), and an abundant bearing in their lives of the fruit produced by God (v. 11).

Conclusion

Johann Sebastian Bach was perhaps the greatest composer of history. Bach had two consuming loves in his life: music and God.

As with most geniuses, Bach wasn't much appreciated in his day. His close neighbors thought little more of him than they did of the local merchant or the shoe cobbler, and his sons did little but criticize him.

When Bach died in 1750 he was buried in an unmarked grave in a Leipzig, Germany, churchyard. It took dedicated musicians forty-six years just to collect all the music he had written, and it filled sixty huge printed volumes when the task was completed.

In his book *If with All Your Heart,* Roy O. McClain declared that it would take a music copyist seventy years just to write down the scores the way Bach wrote them. But Bach also composed them as well!

"Did he really live?" McClain asked. He then told how Bach

began to compose at nine. Living with a tyrannical, older brother, Bach was denied the use of his brother's musical library. Bach, however, would slip into the library after everyone else was asleep and copy music by moonlight. After he had completed copying by hand every note of instrumental music in the library, his brother found it and burned it!

But Bach didn't give up. He continued to compose great music, living in life's major key! He refused to major on minors, and as a result he has left to the world a musical legacy that will live for centuries.

He set a good pattern for musicians to emulate, just as Paul, by his life and teachings, has set a good example for all of us Christians to follow who would not major on minors.

2
Lessons Learned After Dark

(Phil. 1:12-25)

Introduction

During the first World War when it was impossible to import the beautiful singing canaries from their native Harz Mountains of Germany, a canary dealer in New York City developed a method to train domestic canaries to sing.

Walter B. Knight wrote in *Knight's Master Book of New Illustrations,* that using a recording of the beautiful songs of some of the few Harz Mountain canaries he still had, the dealer taught these domestic canaries to sing. And he did it in a unique way. Covering the bird cages with a thick cloth to shut out all the light, he then turned on the record player and taught the canaries to sing in the dark.

There are some songs we learn to sing only in life's dark times. During life's daylight hours, when we are lighthearted and full of life, we don't take time to listen. But when life's sun sets in some sorrow or difficult experience, God gets our attention and in the darkness He teaches us some lessons we need to learn.

The shadows had fallen upon Paul. He was a prisoner of the Roman government. He knew the Philippians loved him and were praying for him because Epaphroditus had told him so. For Paul the sun had set, temporarily, the darkness had descended, and nightfall had come.

But the darkness will not defeat the Almighty One. He would work even in it and teach Paul some lessons that would bless not only the Philippians but all believers in the ages to come.

Life will not always be sweet and joyous. But as we walk with faith in God, life's dark hours will not defeat us. There are some lessons that God will teach us even in the darkness.

God Can Put a Silver Lining in Every Dark Cloud

In her poem "Keep the Home Fires Burning," Lena Guilbert Ford has an interesting thought: "There's a silver lining / Through the dark clouds shining."

Though Paul was a prisoner surrounded by dark, uncertain clouds, he found the silver lining God had put on the dark clouds:

> Now I want you to know, brothers, that what has happened to me has really served to advance the gospel. As a result, it has become clear throughout the whole palace guard and to everyone else that I am in chains for Christ (vv. 12-13).

After carefully thinking through his problems, Paul came to the steadfast conclusion that "what has happened" to him was producing good fruit. "What has happened" could literally be translated, "the things dominating me." Nothing ever "just happens" to the believer. Things either come directly from God or in His permissive will He permits to come. We are controlled neither by fate nor luck.

Paul wanted the Philippians to understand that the things dominating his life—namely his imprisonment—would neither curtail his ministry nor the spread of the gospel. Rather, his dark cloud had a silver lining and his imprisonment "has really served to advance the gospel" (v. 12).

Paul's imprisonment, which Satan planned to use to short-circuit Paul's preaching ministry, was instead being used by God to spread the gospel of redemption.

For months Paul lived in his own rented quarters in Rome. He was chained to a Roman soldier day and night. The guards were changed every few hours, and these pagan guards heard the gospel of Jesus from the lips of the apostle.

The soldiers who guarded the apostle were not just ordinary soldiers. They were the Praetorian Guard. A. T. Roberston wrote that during the reign of Emperor Tiberius there were 10,000 of these handpicked soldiers. "They had double pay and special privileges and became so powerful that the emperors had to court their favour. Paul had contact with one after another of these soldiers."[1]

Chained to these palace guards, Paul had opportunity to witness to Rome's most elite soldiers, many of whom would be saved and, in turn, become missionaries to the ends of the earth where they would be stationed.

During one of his most difficult experiences, as the darkness of uncertainty settled around him in his prison, Paul learned, again, that God gives a silver lining to every dark cloud. This is what he meant when he wrote: "And we know that in all things God works for the good of those who love him, who have been called according to his purpose" (Rom. 8:28).

Think of the great blessings that have come to the world as the result of hardships some have suffered. These blessings are silver linings on otherwise dark clouds.

Sir Walter Scott was physically lame and, consequently, was not as active as other boys his age. But out of these difficulties came *Ivanhoe* and *The Lady of the Lake*.

Abraham Lincoln suffered from poverty with almost no opportunity for a formal education. But because these hardships, Lincoln was able to empathize with the common, hurting people of his day so much so that he became known as "the great commoner."

Benjamin Disraeli, elected to the House of Commons in 1837, was a Jew who suffered from racial prejudice. He was such a poor speaker that when he stood the first time to speak in the House of Commons, he was laughed down by his colleagues. But his dark cloud had a silver lining. Disraeli was the only Jew in history ever elected Prime Minister of Great Britain.

Scottish author Robert Louis Stevenson, suffering from tuberculosis, moved to the South Pacific in an attempt to regain his health. He didn't find health there, but he did find the inspiration to write poetry and novels loved by young and old alike. His cloud had a silver lining.

Louis Pasteur was lame in one leg and suffered a stroke in his adult years, but his dark cloud had a silver lining. Refusing to give up, Pasteur developed the process by which children could be immunized against killer diseases.

Beethoven's increasing deafness did not stop him from hearing great symphonies in his mostly quiet world and then putting those great symphonies down on paper to bless millions.

Handel's depression and sense of failure became the catalyst that drove him to write the *Messiah*. Edison's near deafness from childhood was a major factor, he said, in helping him concentrate in his quiet world. John Bunyan's twelve-year imprisonment in Bedford's jail produced *The Pilgrim's Progress*, one of the greatest, most popular books ever written.

One of the lessons we learn when the darkness descends upon us is that God can put a silver lining on every dark cloud.

God Can Use Our Problems to Encourage Others

Because of my chains, most of the brothers in the Lord have been encouraged to speak the word of God more courageously and fearlessly. It is true that some preach Christ out of envy and rivalry, but other out of goodwill. The latter do so in love, knowing that I am put here for the defense of the gospel. The former preach Christ out of selfish ambition, not sincerely, supposing that they can stir up trouble for me while I am in chains. But what does it matter? The most important thing is that in every way, whether from false motives or true, Christ is preached, and because of this I rejoice. Yes, and I will continue to rejoice (vv. 14-18).

Roman persecution of the Christians was not yet severe or widespread. Ominous signs foretold its coming, but Nero had not yet launched his wholesale attack upon the followers of Christ.

But Paul's presence in Rome, although as a prisoner, was a source of encouragement to the believers there. His boldness in preaching the gospel, and his witnessing to his Roman captors and visitors, gave courage to the Roman believers.

Paul's courageous example was encouraging "most of the

brothers in the Lord . . . to speak the world of God more coura-geously and fearlessly" (v. 14).

There are always those who play it safe and then there are the risk takers. The same is true in the Christian life. In Rome, there were some courageous believers who faithfully shared the gospel without concern for their safety, but there were also those who were timid and withdrawn, fearing they would be found out if they said too much.

But Paul's brave preaching and witnessing had encouraged "most of the brethren." As Robertson put it:

> "The most of the brethren" constituted that inner circle of the brother-hood that does and dares things for Christ while the rest hang back. Paul was lucky to have won a majority to this scale of activity. It is usually the minority of Christians who put energy into the work while the majority drift along or criticize what the minority do.[2]

Paul's courage had shamed those who were timid into greater boldness, and it had encouraged the bold ones to witness with greater conviction and joy.

> Some, never eloquent before, now find tongues of angels as they catch the spirit of Paul. The bolder spirits were rendered "more abun-dantly bold" than they were before. These cast caution to the winds and are overwhelming daring in their championship of Jesus.[3]

God was at work and Satan would not defeat the eternal pur-poses of God. He would even use Paul's imprisonment to hasten the spread of the gospel. Paul's problems would produce sweet fruit!

The apostle's courageous testimony had stirred some of the be-lievers up to "preach Christ out of envy and rivalry." It had stirred others up to preach Christ "out of goodwill" (v. 15).

One group preached because it was envious of Paul's success. These may have been, as Robertson suggested, "the old teachers of the church in Rome who did not relish Paul's leadership since it dis-places them, a form of jealousy that one sees only too often."[4]

Or, these may have been the Jews, as Wuest suggested, who

preached that conformance to Moses's law was the door to Christianity. Their real goal was to advance Judaism, not the gospel of the Galilean.

To Paul it didn't matter which group was preaching Christ. Certainly, it mattered to him that the full and clear message of Jesus was not being declared by some, but Paul lays that aside to rejoice in the fact that "in every way, whether from false motives or true, Christ is preached" (v. 18). He found joy in knowing that Jesus is preached.

The lesson here is clear: God often uses the problems that envelop us to encourage others in life's struggles. And, certainly, He uses the problems Christians face victoriously to encourage other Christians to live courageously and victoriously.

What we owe to the encouragement of others can never be calculated. All of us have been encouraged in some difficult experience of life, by the encouragement of others, to press on and not give up.

A. J. Cronin was one of these. Born in Scotland in 1896, he took his medical degree from the University of Glasgow and served as a surgeon in World War I. When Cronin was a medical student, his surgical skills were severely criticized by one of his professors. And Cronin had a hard time getting over it.

"You do not have the skills to become a surgeon," the teacher told Cronin. "You would be well advised to give up the idea of being a surgeon and settle for being a general practitioner."

Cronin believed what his professor said, and in discouragement he gave up the idea of becoming a surgeon. After completing medical school at Glasgow, he went to a remote village in the Highlands of Scotland and there, as the only doctor for many miles around, he opened his office.

Physician A. Dudley Dennison, Jr. wrote in his book *Windows, Ladders, and Bridges,* that one cold winter day a pastor in the area was seriously injured when a tree fell on him. Cronin knew that unless a delicate surgical procedure was done immediately, the pastor would be paralyzed. But he also remembered what his professor in medical school had told him: "You do not have the skills to be surgeon."

Cronin wrestled with what he should do. He knew that one

mistake could mean complete paralysis or maybe even instant death for the pastor. But the pastor encouraged the young doctor to perform the needed surgery. "I will pray as you operate," the pastor said. And encouraged by the pastor, Cronin performed the surgery and the pastor recovered. It was the pastor's encouragement that made the difference for Cronin, and his confidence was restored.

Often we have been encouraged by the way others have handled their problems. We have learned from them.

Napoleon's military tactics have been studied for generations by military strategists. But Napoleon came from humble, poor people and his early years were a terrible struggle.

Millions have been encouraged by the struggles of fellow sufferers: Daniel Defoe wrote *Robinson Crusoe* while in prison. John Bunyan produced *The Pilgrim's Progress* because of prison. Sir Walter Raleigh wrote *The History of the World* during thirteen years in jail. Luther translated the Bible while imprisoned in the castle at Wartburg. Dante wrote magnificently during his twenty years in prison, part of the time under a death sentence.

Who has not found encouragement in John Milton? Blind, sick, poor, he refused to give up. "Who best can suffer, best can do," Milton said.

And don't forget Lord Byron when you are about defeated. He was clubfooted and severely criticized for his first work, "Hours of Idleness," which was published when he was only nineteen. But Byron, for all his wickedness, was acclaimed one of England's great poets before he died at age thirty-seven.

One of the lessons God teaches us when the darkness falls upon us is that He can use our problems to encourage others. Did He not so use Paul?

God Can Give Us Sufficient Courage for
Every Situation We Face

For I know that through your prayers and the help given by the Spirit of Jesus Christ, what has happened to me will turn out for my deliverance. I eagerly expect and hope that I will in no way be ashamed, but will have sufficient courage so that now as always Christ will be exalted in my body, whether by life or by death. For to me, to live is Christ and to die is gain (vv. 19-21).

This is not the whimper of one who is defeated. Rather, it is the shout of a victor. Paul tells the Philippians that it matters little what the Romans do to him. Already much good has come from his sufferings. And he knows that Christ will give him strength and courage for every problem that lies ahead.

His release from prison is not his primary concern. His chief concern is "that I will in no way be ashamed" (v. 20). He will be sustained in every trial through the prayers of the Philippians and "the help" (v. 19) that the Holy Spirit provides.

Glorifying Jesus is primary. As Frank Stagg put it: "He wants to meet his fate, whether life or death, with such dignity and spirit that all may see what Christ means to him."[5]

"For to me, to live is Christ and to die is gain" (v. 21), is one of Paul's best-known statements. Christ had given meaning to Paul's life. Death held no terror for Paul. Whether he lived or died was entirely up to Jesus Christ. God will give Paul courage and faith whichever way it goes.

Multitudes of Christians through the centuries have read these moving words of Paul and have found courage and new faith in them, for they are a resounding testimony to the God of sufficiency! When some problem has been almost too heavy to bear, or when some crisis or sorrow has all but squeezed the life out of us, many of us have read these words and have gone back to face life with fresh courage.

Conclusion

Sub pondere cresco—"I grow under the burden"—is the motto of one of the Scottish clans. Indeed! If we Christians learn the lessons darkness teaches, we shall grow in Christlikeness. But if we don't, our lives will forever be spiritually stunted for much of life is spent in dark and shadowy places.

Notes

1. A. T. Roberston, "The Epistles of Paul," vol. IV, *Word Pictures in the New Testament* (Nashville: Broadman Press, 1979), 438.

2. A. T. Robertson, *Paul's Joy in Christ* (Nashville: Broadman Press), 79.

3. Ibid, 80.

4. Ibid, 82.

5. Frank Stagg, *The Broadman Bible Commentary,* Vol. 11, "2 Corinthians—Philemon" (Nashville: Broadman Press, 1971), 190.

3
Spoonfuls of Sunshine

(Phil. 1:19-26)

Introduction

In Dic Browne's comic strip "Hi and Lois," little Trixie is still at the crawling stage. Some of Trixie's best friends are sunbeams and Browne often draws Trixie either talking to a sunbeam or playing with one.

Trixie reminds me of a children's story I read years ago. One morning while young Johnny was eating breakfast—more playing than eating—a sparkling, golden sunbeam fell across the table and into his plate. With his spoon, Johnny reached out toward the sunbeam and acted as though he were scooping it up. Then putting the spoon to his mouth, he playfully exclaimed to his mother: "Mommy! Mommy! Look, I've eaten a spoonful of sunshine!"

The stories of Trixie and Johnny are really not too infantile for us adults. There is a message in them we would do well to remember: more than anything else, we need sunshine in our lives.

But I am not talking about the sunshine that comes down from the sun. Rather, I mean the spiritual sunshine of courage, cheerfulness, joy, and optimism that come down from heaven. That is the kind of sunshine our world desperately needs. And, thanks be to God, we can have it.

Paul had it. Even as a Roman prisoner he lived in the sunshine. Although he had been Nero's prisoner for four long years, he had not given up. He wasn't groping in the darkness. He had found the key to life, and he was living in the sunshine!

Here are three spoonfuls of sunshine that I want to share with you. If we accept them and live by them, they are sure to brighten our lives.

We Must Get Our Priorities Straight

Listen to Paul's testimony in verses 20-21: "Always Christ will be exalted in my body, whether by life or by death. For to me, to live is Christ and to die is gain."

Paul is saying that whether he lives or dies is not the main issue. He has his priorities straight and is determined to glorify Jesus in whatever comes. His relationship with Jesus is so intimate that the two are inseparable. For Paul to continue to live and serve is for Jesus to live through him. Paul admits, however, that it would be to his advantage to go on home to heaven to be with Jesus.

The late R. G. Lee was the beloved pastor of the Bellevue Baptist Church of Memphis, Tennessee. He was one of the best-known and most powerful preachers of this century. When I was a pastor in Mississippi, I invited Dr. Lee to come one weekend and preach in our church. Never shall I forget it. On Sunday morning, at my request, he preached on heaven. On Sunday night he brought his immortal sermon "Payday Someday" that he had preached more than twelve hundred times all over the nation.

As we sat at breakfast on Sunday morning, I listened to the great preacher as he talked about things spiritual, when the opportunity presented itself. I asked Dr. Lee how real Jesus was to him. Pointing to a nearby chair, the old saint replied: "He is just as real to me as that chair."

That is what Paul was saying. Jesus was so real to Paul that for him to live would be for Jesus to live. Long ago, Paul had settled the matter of who would be first in his life.

Paul settled the question on the Damascus Road some years before he wrote this letter (Acts 9). On his way from Jerusalem to Damascus to persecute Christians, this devout Jew met Jesus Christ in a startling and miraculous way. There Jesus rearranged Paul's priorities. As he yielded to the Savior, Jesus saved him, called him to preach, and filled his life with spiritual sunshine. And Paul was never the same again.

This commitment to Jesus gave Paul a deep sense of security as he faced the life-and-death issues of prison: "If I am to go on living in the body, this will mean fruitful labor for me. Yet what shall I choose? I do not know!" (v. 22).

Paul confessed it would be far better for him to depart and be with Christ, but he conceded that it would be better for them if he were spared so he could continue to teach them and minister to them.

But whatever befell him, he was ready for it. His priorities were straight. Whatever it cost him, his mind was made up. He will stand firm: "Now as always Christ will be exalted in my body, whether by life or by death" (v. 20).

It's a radiant, glorious, and large spoonful of sunshine that the apostle served up here! Out of his own experience he told us that our lives will be happier and brighter if we decide today who will be first in our lives. Doing this is guaranteed to bring heaven's sunshine into one's life.

We Live for Something Bigger Than Ourselves

Paul shows us in verses 22-24 that he was living for something bigger than himself: "If I am to go on living in the body, this will mean fruitful labor for me. Yet what shall I choose? I do not know! I am torn between the two: I desire to depart and be with Christ, which is better by far; but it is more necessary for you that I remain in the body."

Here is a man who had come to the end of himself. Pride and selfish ambition no longer drove him. Once they did, but when he met Jesus on the road Paul was so challenged by Jesus to live for something bigger than himself that it had revolutionized his life, even as it will revolutionize our lives.

An elderly gentleman prided himself on his ability as an art critic. Although he was very nearsighted, that didn't keep him from giving his opinion on art at every opportunity. One day when he and his wife went with some friends to a large art gallery, the man seized his chance.

Standing before a large framed portrait, he launched into his treatise on art.

"In the first place," he said, "this frame is not in keeping with the subject. The frame is entirely too large for the face. As for the subject himself, he is far too homely to make a good picture."

"Psst" hissed his wife as she edged her way toward him. "Psst, John, psst," she kept hissing. But John was so caught up in his role of art critic that he never heard her.

"It's a great mistake for any artist to choose so homely a subject for a picture. He can never expect to paint a masterpiece with such an ugly subject." And, again, from behind him came the sound of his imploring, concerned wife: "John, psst, psst," she whispered.

By now her calls were frantic. But John plowed on. He would have these poor dumbbells know just how sophisticated and urbane he was.

"Now," John continued authoritatively, "if the artist had chosen a face with at least some character in it his picture would be so much better."

"Psst, psst, John," his wife called again. By now she was at his side. Finally getting his attention, she whispered in his ear: "For Pete's sake, John, shut up! You're looking in a mirror!"

The Christian whose focus is all inward, who spends his time and energies wondering how to impress others and draw more attention to himself, will never live the full life. Jesus told us that we would find our life only by giving it away (Matt. 10:39).

Paul was well aware of this. For years he had been giving himself away to others in the name of Jesus Christ. This holy challenge to live for Jesus and the gospel had so revolutionized Paul that even as he faced possible death there was no fear.

He looked at life's two great ultimates: to go on living or to die. Whether he lived or died was not up to him, but he said that if it were, it would be far better to die and go home to be with Jesus.

Paul had become the slave of Jesus. He had given up his will for the will of his Master. Living now for someone and something bigger than himself, Paul had come to the settled conclusion that to stay alive and to minister in the name of Jesus is the better of the two choices. And as Beethoven said when deafness settled over him, Paul took life by the throat and moved on!

When Henry David Thoreau moved away from civilization in 1845 to live in peace at Walden Pond, he wrote: "It will be a success if I shall have left myself behind."

That's the key! God's glorious sunshine fills and floods the lives of those who live unselfishly for Him and others.

We Must Face Life with Optimism

Listen to Paul's ringing exclamation of optimism. It rattles the chain on his arm and startles the guard chained to the other end:

> Convinced of this, I know that I will remain, and I will continue with all of you for your progress and joy in the faith, so that through my being with you again your joy in Christ Jesus will overflow on account of me (vv. 25-26).

He was a prisoner. It was a hard time for him. Things looked dark. He knew he must yet stand before Nero. He knew his life hung in the balance. But this courageous preacher also knew that Jesus was still on the throne. Christ had given Paul faith for the dark hours. He had prayed the matter through, and he refused to be defeated. Paul, therefore, determined to face the future with optimism and faith.

When W. A. Criswell was eighteen years old and a student at Baylor University in Waco, Texas, he was called to be pastor of the First Baptist Church of Devil's Bend, Texas. It was a church with forty-one members.

Criswell said there was an old potbellied stove in the middle of the room where the church met for worship. Many of the men chewed tobacco back then, and they would chew until they were about to drown, Criswell said. Then, right in the middle of the service, they would get up, unhook the stove door and spit, sometimes nearly putting out the fire! But Criswell said he would preach on. However, he longed for the day when he would be the pastor of a church that had brass cuspidors.

Billy Keith, Criswell's biographer, wrote that according to Criswell on Saturday afternoons the church at Devil's Bend held its business meeting. The "againers" were always there and seated in full force on the front row.

Dr. Criswell told how one Saturday a member stood up and said, "My brothers, I make a motion we build a fence around the cemetery."

Another member stood up and shouted, "I'm against it!"

When the "againer" was asked why he was against the fence, he gave his reason: "Do you know anybody in the cemetery who can get out? Do you know anybody on the outside who wants to get in? Why, then, should we build a fence around the cemetery?"

Some Christians live as though they want to get into the cemetery, or are already there! Filled with pessimism, defeated, joyless, nothing ever seems to go right for them. Everybody is against them. Whipped and discouraged, they drag through life with heavy steps and long faces. Like Mr. Muckrake in *The Pilgrim's Progress*, they go through life with downcast eyes hardly ever looking up. And that's about the best way I know to wind up permanently in the cemetery!

Paul learned that he could not live well or effectively unless he clung to an optimistic outlook on life. But his optimism was not shallow. It is based on faith in Jesus Christ. Though Paul had been a prisoner for four long years, his voice still rung with optimism: "I know that I will remain, and I will continue with all of you for your progress and joy in the faith" (v. 25). That's no whimper of one who is defeated!

We must learn the lesson Paul learned. We have the choice. We can face life defeated or with courage. The choice is up to us. But looking at life through dark glasses won't improve it one degree. Actually, it will work against us.

Facing the hard realities of life in faith and optimism will help us handle whatever life may hurl against us. Our work will go better. Our play will be better. Our night's rest will be better. And life will take on an aura of brightness and sunshine that we never thought possible.

The choice is ours. Both the sunshine and the shadows, beckon, and we will cast the deciding vote where we shall live. But God is waiting to fill our lives with His wonderful, powerful sunshine of love and grace if only we will let Him.

Conclusion

Jesus can change our dreary, defeated, sin-chained lives, fill us with His Holy Spirit and the radiant, victorious spiritual sunshine He gives. But we must let Him.

Norman Vincent Peale told about a Mrs. Charles Philipia who had the ambition to walk from New York City to Miami, Florida. It was a most difficult undertaking, but she did it.

When she reached Miami and was asked by a reporter how she managed to do it, she said all she had to do was take one step at a time. After she took the first step, which was the hardest step of all, she took another and another.

The same thing is true for those of us who would live above the dismal shadows of life. To walk on the sunny side of life begins with the first step: unreserved commitment to our Lord Jesus Christ. After that step, it's sunshine all the way even when the shadows fall!

4
Pilgrims Here but Citizens There!

(Phil. 1:27-30)

Introduction

A Unitarian minister in Birmingham, Michigan, set a new record for the longest sermon ever preached. He preached for sixty hours and thirty-one minutes—six minutes longer than the old record. His subject was "From Abraham to Augustine," and dealt with religious history.

As he neared the end of his marathon sermon, the minister signaled to the few hardy people who were still with him that he was about to finish. Suddenly, one of his listeners shouted, "At least make your point!"

Can you imagine it? A man who had no gospel to preach preached for sixty hours and thirty-one minutes, and still he hadn't made his point. He talked and talked and talked. If he ever had a point, he never made it!

As we look at this passage of Scripture, it is apparent that Paul made his point. It isn't a marathon sermon, but one that consists of only four verses. Yet in these four brief verses, he reminded the Philippian believers from his prison in Rome that they were only pilgrims here on earth but citizens of heaven.

Since this is the case, Paul told the Philippians, and us, how to live. Three things, he wrote, are involved: we must watch behavior; we must guard our attitudes, and we must seize our opportunities.

We Must Watch Our Behavior

"Whatever happens, conduct yourself in a manner worthy of the gospel of Christ" (v. 27).

In the preceding verses, Paul shared with the Philippians how he felt about his future. He hoped and prayed that he would be released to return and encourage them in their faith. But whether he did was not really the most important thing. Paul's priority, stated in verse 20, is that "Christ will be exalted in my body, whether by life or by death."

In verse 27 he speaks of "Whatever happens." He believed that through their prayers he would be freed and restored to them, but "whatever happens" they were to live as Christ would have them live. They were to conduct themselves "in a manner worthy of the gospel of Christ."

The word "conduct" is translated in the *King James Version* by the word "conversation." But when the *King James Version* was translated in 1611, the word *conversation* meant, "manner of life, behavior." But today it means to talk to someone about something. Our word *politics* is derived from this Greek word.

A. T. Robertson wrote:

> The life of Paul in Rome had made him think afresh of the great Roman empire; he himself was a Roman citizen (Acts 22:28) by birth and was proud of it. From the great center of the Roman world he would naturally think of Christianity in Roman terms, as Jesus so often spoke of the kingdom of God, a Jewish conception. But the Philippians themselves lived in a city that was a Roman colony and so were perfectly familiar with the rights and dignity of Roman citizenship. Clement of Rome also . . . shows how Christians owe obligations to a spiritual polity as citizens do to the state. Christians are to live worthily of the Gospel of Christ. This is the standard.[1]

Paul was telling the Philippians that although they were citizens of the heavenly kingdom, they were also citizens of the Roman Empire. They were to watch their behavior and live in such a manner that they will magnify their heavenly citizenship. Their lives—our lives—must complement the gospel of Jesus.

He says we are to conduct ourselves "in a manner worthy of the gospel of Christ." "Conduct" also means "having the same weight" or "weighing as much as." Our life is to weigh as much as the profession we make as Christians. If we say we are Christians, then our lives must measure up to our claim. In other words, we must walk our talk!

Most of us who are past forty remember the logo on the old RCA Victor records: a dog listening attentively to the sound coming from an old phonograph speaker. For years I wondered what that picture symbolized. Sometime ago I found out.

In his booklet *Live Sermon Outlines*, Ian MacPherson tells about it. In 1877, when Thomas A. Edison invented the phonograph, Francis Barraud was living in the south of England. He had a dog named Nipper and, impressed with Edison's new invention, Barraud painted a picture of his dog attentively listening to a record being played on the phonograph.

After Barraud had finished his painting, he sent it to a company in the United States that was producing the phonograph. Barraud titled his painting, "His Master's Voice," and suggested that the company might want to use it for a logo.

The company turned down Barraud's offer, for it wasn't impressed. But thirty years later, the phonograph was replaced by the gramophone and Barraud changed his painting just a little and sent it back to the company. They accepted his painting and Nipper made Barraud wealthy.

Paul is telling us Christians that because we are citizens of the heavenly kingdom we must listen to our Master's voice—we must watch our behavior—and live in a way that shows to others we are followers of Jesus.

Martin Luther once said that if someone should knock on the door of his heart and ask, "Who lives here?" that he would not reply, "Luther lives here." Rather, he would reply, "Jesus lives here."

We must live in such a manner that when a questioning world looks at us and wonders why we live as we do, it will have no problem finding the answer. We live as we do because Christ lives within us.

Since we are only pilgrims here but citizens there, not only must we watch our behavior, but also:

We Must Guard Our Attitudes

Attitude is of major importance in everything. Our attitude will determine the kind of life we live. Those who know about such things say that one's attitude is probably the most important thing necessary for success.

In his book *Shadows We Run From,* Nelson Price wrote that the Carnegie Institute once analyzed the lives of 10,000 people and determined that only 50 percent of success is due to technical training and that 85 percent of success is due to personality. The single most important personality trait listed was attitude. Following attitude were thoroughness, observation, creative imagination, and decision.

Paul underscores here the importance of Christians showing the right attitude. He declares that one way it will express itself is by our standing "firm in one spirit, contending as one man for the faith of the gospel without being frightened in any way by those who oppose you" (vv. 27-28).

Several positive things about a Christian's attitude were listed here by Paul:

We Are To Stand Firm

It is easy to stand tall when things are easy. But it is a different matter to stand tall when it is hard and costly. Paul's picture is that of a Roman soldier standing his ground against the enemy. As a good soldier stands his ground when it is difficult to do so, Christians are to be true to the Savior and His teachings even when it is unpopular and costly.

We Are To Be United

"Stand firm in one spirit, contending as one man for the faith of the gospel" (v. 27). A. T. Robertson wrote: "Teamwork in the games is absolutely essential. . . . Paul knew the spirit of the athletic games, and made frequent use of metaphors from them."[2]

The Philippian church was being told to stand together, and

contend together, as though they were one person. Epaphroditus had brought word that the church was divided, and Paul was exhorting the believers to work together in unity and coordination as though they were one person. How this exhortation is needed today with the division and disunity that exist in so many churches!

They Are To Be Courageous

"Without being frightened in any way by those who oppose you" (v. 28). Fear of their adversaries must be overcome by prayer and faith. Courage in the face of opposition must replace any fear they might have as they live where it is costly to be a Christian.

"Frightened," A. T. Robertson declared in his book *Paul's Joy in Christ,* is a word used to describe a horse that has been startled or a bird that has suddenly been flushed into flight. As horses that will stand still amid booming cannons and bursting shells, Christians must live fearlessly and courageously for Christ in the midst of difficulties. "This refusal to be flustered is proof to the adversaries of their eternal destruction and of your eternal salvation. And this proof comes from God,"[3] Robertson wrote.

Through the centuries millions of Christians have done just this. Even facing certain death for their convictions, they have been faithful to Jesus. The church today needs to reclaim this courageous spirit. The quitters and compromisers will never get the gospel of redemption out to a lost world. Only faithful Christians who neither quit nor compromise will get the job done.

Dietrich Bonhoeffer was one of those courageous Christians. Donald T. Kauffman told in his book *For Instance,* that when the Second World War broke out, Bonhoeffer was safe at Union Theological Seminary in New York City. But when this young German theologian saw what was happening to his homeland, he returned to Germany to stand with his people against Adolph Hitler. Again and again Bonhoeffer spoke out against the Nazi regime. Framed and arrested by the Nazis who charged him with conspiring to kill Hitler, they hanged Bonhoeffer at the age of thirty-nine.

But before the Nazis murdered him, Bonhoeffer left behind a

legacy of faith in his book *The Cost of Discipleship*. There he wrote about Christians who will not shrink in fear even when it is desperately costly to follow Jesus.

Attitudes control Christian behavior! Therefore, Paul tells us to guard our attitudes.

But there is one final thought here that we must see. Since we are only pilgrims on earth but citizens of the heavenly kingdom:

We Must Seize Our Opportunities

"For it has been granted to you on behalf of Christ not only to believe on him, but also to suffer for him, since you are going through the same struggle you saw I had, and now hear that I still have" (vv. 29-30).

Paul listed here two great opportunities or privileges that are given to every Christian. The words he uses describe these opportunities as special gifts of grace given to us by our Lord.

We Have the Opportunity To Believe in Christ

"For it has been granted you on behalf of Christ not only to believe on him" (v. 29). Trusting in Christ as our Savior, and trusting in Christ to sustain us, is not something forced upon us. Rather, it is "granted" to us by faith through the grace of God.

No opportunity in this world is higher or nobler or more to be desired than the privilege of trusting in Jesus as one's Savior. Believing upon Christ to save us is our only recourse if we are to be saved from sin and hell. And believing upon Christ to sustain us is our only sufficient resource if we are to live victoriously for him.

In *Julius Caesar*, William Shakespeare made a striking statement that deals with opportunity:

> There is a tide in the affairs of men,
> Which, taken at the flood, leads on to fortune;
> Omitted, all the voyage of their life
> Is bound in shallows and in miseries.

The opportunity to believe in Christ certainly "leads on to fortune." But when neglected, life "is bound in shallows and in miseries."

But there is a second opportunity that Christ offers to us.

We Have the Opportunity To Suffer for Him

"For it has been granted to you on behalf of Christ, . . . also to suffer for him" (v. 29). Evangelist Billy Graham says that more Christians have suffered and died for Christ in the twentieth century than in any century, including the early centuries of Christian persecution. Any careful researcher of modern Christian history knows that in godless countries around the world millions of believers have suffered greatly for their faith. And multitudes still do.

Paul's writing about suffering for Jesus seems rather strange to us, doesn't it? Christians in America don't pay much in a personal way for the privilege of being a Christian. We are protected by laws written into the Bill of Rights that guarantee our religious freedom.

But there is a price that every committed believer pays for his faith. Remember what Paul told Timothy: "In fact, everyone who wants to live a godly life in Christ Jesus will be persecuted, while evil men and impostors will go from bad to worse, deceiving and being deceived" (2 Tim. 3:12-13).

Christians who stand up for their Savior, who do not compromise their convictions, who put Jesus first in everything won't be thrown into jail, but they will pay a price for it. They will be talked about, ostracized, and misunderstood. No believer should live offensively, talk foolishly, or live with a long face and sour disposition as though he were a martyr. No, but even Christians who live gently, kindly, and graciously will still suffer to some degree for their faith. It has always been so.

Having listed these two grace-gift opportunities that have been given to the Philippians, Paul encourages them by reminding them of his sufferings for Christ. "Take courage from me," he writes. "I have suffered and am suffering, but I have not denied my Lord."

Conclusion

In the early 1960s, the heroic Christian leader Martin Niemöller came to America on a speaking tour. Knowing of his experience under the Hitler regime and of his resistance to the Nazis, two newspaper reporters hurried to hear him, expecting a sensational discussion of those war years.

After listening to Dr. Niemöller preach a genuine gospel message, they left the church disappointed. One reporter said to the other, "Six years in a Nazi prison camp and all he has to talk about is Jesus Christ."[4]

Why was Niemöller so preoccupied with Jesus that he cared only to talk about Him? It was because his suffering had taught him the worth of things eternal. He knew he was only a suffering pilgrim here but a permanent citizen there!

Notes

1. A. T. Robertson, *Paul's Joy in Christ—Studies in Philippians* (Nashville: Broadman Press, 1979), 103.

2. Ibid, 105.

3. Ibid, 106.

4. James E. Hightower, *Illustrating Paul's Letter to the Romans* (Nashville: Broadman Press, 1984), 113.

5

In the Presence of Greatness

(Phil. 2:5-11)

Introduction

The Battle of Gettysburg marked a turning point in the war between the states. The battle on July 1-3, 1863, involved 165,000 men and left 38,000 casualties.

The next November, President Abraham Lincoln went to Gettysburg, Pennsylvania, to dedicate a portion of that battlefield as a memorial to those who had died there. But Lincoln wasn't the main speaker for the dedication. The main speaker was Edward Everett, a politician and one of the greatest orators of that day.

So moved by Lincoln's ability to say so much in so few words, Everett predicted the President's speech would live for generations while his speech would soon be forgotten. Later, he wrote the President: "I should be glad if I could flatter myself that I came as near to the central idea of the occasion in two hours as you did in two minutes."

Among those who heard Lincoln speak that epochal day was a newspaper editor from Harrisburg, Pennsylvania, thirty-five miles from Gettysburg. In his editorial the editor remarked: "We pass over the silly remarks of the President; for the credit of the nation, we are willing that the veil of oblivion shall be dropped over them and that they shall no more be repeated or thought of."

The poor, foolish, myopic editor! He stood in the presence of greatness and listened to some of the sublimest words ever spoken, but he never heard them.

As we come reverently to this Philippian text, we stand in the presence of greatness. Where, in all Scripture, can one find such a magnificent statement about the person of Jesus Christ as one finds here?

About A.D. 61, during his first Roman imprisonment, Paul wrote these words to the church at Philippi. This was the first church founded by him on the continent of Europe. He loved them devotedly, and they returned his love. But Epaphroditus, one of Paul's fellow workers and a native of Philippi, had brought word to Paul that the sweet fellowship of the church was being threatened by a selfish, proud, self-centered spirit possessed by some of the Philippian believers.

In rebuking their haughty spirit, Paul cited the humility of Jesus that was demonstrated by His incarnation and death. Then, pleading for them to walk humbly before God and with each other, Paul wrote: "Your attitude should be the same as that of Christ Jesus" (v. 5).

In the passage that follows, the apostle gave us the grandest statement about Christ in the Scriptures.

The Eternal Christ

Paul began his magnificent statement about Christ by taking us back into the eons of eternity before time began. Creation's first morning has not yet dawned. But Paul wrote about Christ: "Who, being in very nature God, did not consider equality with God something to be grasped" (v. 6).

This is the preexistent, eternal Christ. He has not yet been born, but He is alive in all his glory with the Father in eternity. Paul's words are clear: "Back then in eternity Christ possessed the very nature of God." His words are reminiscent of John 1.

"Who, being in very nature God" are very instructive about the preincarnate nature of Christ. "Being" describes a past eternal state extended into time. In eternity Christ possessed the very nature of God, and in His incarnation He still possessed that nature.

In eternity, His "very nature" was that of "God" (v. 6). With the

Father before time began He possessed and expressed the divine essence.

In eternity Christ knew that He was God, and the angels knew that He was God. "Holy! Holy! Holy!" had been the anthem of praise they had sung to Him long before Bethlehem's manger. But contrary to the haughty, selfish spirit being expressed by the quarreling Philippians, Jesus did not react haughtily or selfishly to His place of preeminence. "[He] did not consider equality with God something to be grasped"—that is held on to at all costs (v. 6, see also John 17:5).

The Earthly Christ

Paul moved now to the incarnation of Christ. He who was always the Son of God now becomes the Son of man: "But made himself nothing, taking the very nature of a servant, being made in human likeness" (v. 7).

The incarnation was a voluntary thing. Jesus "made himself nothing." It was not forced upon Him. He saw our great need of a Savior, and He responded voluntarily to that need (John 10:17-18). The words "made himself nothing" may literally be translated "emptied himself."

The question arises, of what did Jesus empty Himself in His incarnation? It was not His deity, for in His human flesh He was still God. Rather, He set aside the outward expression of His deity that He had always possessed. Paul tells us what that meant: "Taking the very nature of a servant, being made in human likeness" (v. 7). As the late R. G. Lee was fond of saying: "He was as much God as God is God, but as much man as man is man."

The servant nature that Jesus took is explained by the "human likeness" He took at His birth. He laid aside the outward expression of His deity—the glory, privilege, majesty that had always been His—and was born a baby, grew as a child, and matured as a man (Luke 2:52).

Augustine, the fourth-century church father, called Jesus "The

God man" and that is what Paul is saying here. One of the clearest pictures of this is found in John 13 where "The God man" literally acts out His servant role by washing the disciples' feet.

But "taking the very nature of a servant" was a voluntary thing. All that coerced Jesus was His love for sinners.

Paul tells us in verse 8 how far His love for us extended: "He humbled himself and became obedient to death—even death on a cross!"

Paul seems to catch his breath as he sighs, "Even death on a cross!" Oh! What love divine!

The Exalted Christ

In all literature you will find nothing as majestic as what now follows. Because of Christ's unselfish spirit—and remember the selfish spirit of the Philippians is what Paul was rebuking—in humbling Himself and dying the ignominious death of a criminal, Paul writes "God exalted him to the highest place and gave him the name that is above every name" (v. 9).

Volumes have been written explaining "the name" given to the exalted Christ. I understand it simply to be "The name of Jesus [before which] every knee should bow, in heaven and on earth and under the earth," as Paul writes in verse 10.

Jesus means "Jehovah saves." It was given to Him prophetically before He was born, for He would be the one who would "save his people from their sins" (Matt. 1:21). He died, was raised from the dead, and is now seated at the Father's right hand. That name which was given to Him prophetically is now earned by Him actually as He fulfills the prophecies about His death, burial, and resurrection. He who was named Savior by the angel has earned that name by His sacrifice.

Using this magnificent demonstration of humility and self-emptying love by Him who is above all in heaven or on earth, Paul pleaded with the haughty, quarreling Philippians to lay aside their pride and walk humbly with each other.

Conclusion

Roland Hayes, the gifted black tenor, was born in what had been slave quarters in Georgia and reared in poverty. He did not know who his father was and grew up with almost no advantages. But Hayes had a Christian mother who helped make a difference.

J. Ralph Grant, in his book *The Word of the Lord for Special Days,* wrote that doors began to open for Hayes after a teacher from Oberlin Conservatory of Music heard him sing. And before the end of his distinguished career, Hayes sang before thousands of people including the king of England.

Nervous because of his appointment to sing at Buckingham Palace, Hayes cabled his mother for encouragement. The message she wired back to London consisted of only one sentence: "Remember who you are." But it was enough. His mother's words brought to Hayes the poise he needed to perform magnificently before England's king.

In this passage, Paul tells these proud, self-centered Philippians whose church is divided by their quarrelsome spirit to remember who they are: the spiritual beneficiaries of Him who, though above all people and things, humbly laid aside His glory to save them from their sins.

To encourage them to live humbly before God and with each other and to be done with their self-centered pride that has begun to destroy the fellowship of their church, Paul cites the selflessness and humility of Jesus that brought Him from heaven to earth to be our Savior.

For us today, Christ's example of humility and love is a call for us to follow His example in our attitudes toward each other.

6

The Name Above All

(Phil. 2:9-11)

Introduction

English poet Robert Browning told an interesting story about Charles Lamb, another English writer.

Lamb and some of his friends were talking one day when someone asked: "Gentlemen, what would you do if John Milton entered this room?"

Someone quickly replied: "We would give him such an ovation as might compensate for the tardy recognition accorded him by the men of his day."

Someone else then asked, "And, what would you do if Shakespeare entered?"

Another person spoke up: "We would arise and crown him master of song."

A third friend then asked: "And if Jesus Christ were to enter this room, what would you do?"

Charles Lamb answered as a reverent hush fell over the room: "We would all fall on our faces."

Through the centuries millions of believers have believed and confessed that the name of Jesus is the name above all. No other name compares to His name.

This is what Paul was writing about in this text. In the preceding verses he dealt with the humiliation of Jesus: He who had always been equal with the Father, laid aside His eternal glory, was born as a baby, lived as a man, and died upon the cross.

This is the humiliation of Jesus. But, Paul didn't let the matter

rest there for there is much more to be said. In verse 9 he adds trium-
phantly: "Therefore God exalted him to the highest place and gave
him the name that is above every name."

Paul had been pleading for unity in the Philippian church. He
told them that their church has become divided because they have
become proud. He cited to them the humility of Jesus and urged
them to follow his example.

Using the example of Jesus, Paul urged them to be done with
their proud, arrogant attitudes that have brought division. Honor,
he pointed out, comes not by exalting themselves over each other
but by humbling themselves before each other.

With this background, there are four things I want to show you
about the name above all.

The Name that Is Given

"Therefore God exalted him to the highest place and gave him
the name that is above every name" (v. 9).

The Greek of the New Testament speaks more emphatically
than does our English. He is not given "a name which is above every
name," as the *King James Version* renders it, but the name that is
above every name. The reference here is not to any name in general,
but the specific name that is given to Jesus by the Heavenly Father.

What name is this that was given to Jesus after His victorious
return to heaven? Well, we are not specifically told. Rather, it is simply called "the name that is above every name."

We cannot be absolutely sure what name Paul has in mind.
Scholars have wrestled with the question for centuries. Some say
Jesus. Others say Jesus Christ. And others say Lord.

One of the common biblical practices was the giving of a new
name to mark a new development in one's life. You will recall that
Abram became Abraham when God made His covenant with him
(Gen. 17:5). Sarai, Abraham's wife, became Sarah when God promised her a son (v. 15). In the Revelation, the risen Christ promises to
give a new name to believers who overcome (Rev. 2:17; 3:12).

Heaven takes note of Christ's victory over sin, death and the grave, and the Father marks the occasion with the giving of a name to His Son that is commensurate with his victory: "And [He] gave him the name that is above every name" (v. 9).

Those who hold to "Lord" as the new name have a good case. Vincent Taylor says that after Jesus' resurrection, "Lord" was the name most often used by the disciples to speak of Him. Scores of times it appears in one form or another.

I am disposed to believe, however, that the exalted name given to our Lord was the name "Jesus." Paul seems to explain in verse 10, "That at the name of Jesus every knee shall bow," what he means by "the name that is above every name" (v. 9).

Although "Lord" is used to identify Jesus more than any other name in the New Testament, as Vincent Taylor wrote in his book *The Names of Jesus*, it appears that "Lord" may be more of a title than a name. But "Jesus" is a name and "Jesus" is His name (Matt. 1:21).

"Jesus" means "Jehovah saves" or "Jehovah is salvation." Our Lord was so named by the angel when he told Joseph: "She will give birth to a son, and you are to give him the name Jesus, because he will save his people from their sins" (Matt. 1:21).

Taylor wrote that the name "Jesus" was a precious name to first-century Christians, expressing a deep feeling of veneration and worship. It is a personal name, he declared, and most significant because of its meaning, "Jehovah saves."

But, it was not an uncommon name in the first century. Josephus mentions about twenty people named Jesus and ten of them lived during the days Jesus lived. But from the second century onward, the name was abandoned by the Jews because of their antagonism to Christianity. Christians also avoided naming their sons "Jesus" (Hebrew, "Joshua") because of their love for the Lord Jesus.

The late R. C. Campbell tells about a character in one of George MacDonald's novels named Joseph Palworth who decided to read through the New Testament.

"I had no definite ideal in the resolve," he said. "It seemed a good thing to do. It would serve towards keeping up my connection in a way with things above. I began, but did not that night get through the first chapter of Matthew. Conscientiously, I read the chapter of genealogy, but when I came to the twenty-first verse and read, 'Thou shalt call his name Jesus: for he shall save his people from their sins,' I fell on my knees. . . . Here was news of One who came from behind the root of sin to deliver me from that in me which made being a bad thing! . . . Suffice it that from that moment I was a student, a disciple."[1]

It seems, however, that the important thing for us to note is that the exalted name which the Father gave to Jesus after His victory over Satan, is a name to be worshiped, venerated, and revered by believers in all times.

The One Who Gives the Name

Look, again, at verse 9: "Therefore God exalted him to the highest place."

We have here a picture of what took place after Christ's victory over sin and death. He was with His disciples for forty days, and then He ascended to the Father: "After he said this, he was taken up before their eyes, and a cloud hid him from their sight" (Acts 1:9).

In Ephesians 4:8, Paul showed us the victorious Savior ascending into the Father's presence: "When he ascended on high, he led captives in his train and gave gifts to men."

It is an ancient picture of a conquering king returning home from battle with the vanquished bound and in chains following him. He parades them before all the people to show that he has gotten victory over his enemies.

Paul pictured Jesus doing that very thing. As He ascends into heaven, He leads captive His spiritual foes, demonstrating before all heaven that He has completed the work He was given to do. It is a pictorial statement that all is finished!

Having done what the Father sent Jesus to do, and having suffered the shame and humiliation of all that men and Satan could do to Him, we are shown the exaltation of Jesus: "Therefore God exalted him" (v. 9).

We are clearly told that the One who bestows this exalted name and position upon Jesus is God the Heavenly Father Himself. It was He who sent Jesus into the world as the atonement for our sin. And it is He who welcomes the Son back home after the work has been completed that God the Father sent Him to do. Now God the Father exalts Him!

When we are told that "God exalted Him," the verb is written in such a manner that it means He has done it once and for all time. That name that has been given to Jesus is an earned name and it is a permanent name. His exalted position is permanent.

That exalted position and name will never again be taken from Him. Once He laid aside His glory to save us, but He has taken back his glory never to lay it aside again! His exalted name is part of that glory. And the Holy One who bestows the name upon Jesus is also a part of that glory!

The saints who died in faith and who went home to heaven before the crucifixion of Jesus watch His crowning. The angels who kept their first estate, who were not cast out of heaven through pride, witness His exaltation. The seraphim and cherubim that crowd the throne always calling out to God, "Holy! Holy! Holy!" witness Jesus' exaltation.

It is God, the Creator of heaven and earth, who gives to Jesus the name that is above all.

The Authority in the Name

"That at the name of Jesus every knee should bow, in heaven and on earth and under the earth, and every tongue confess that Jesus Christ is Lord, to the glory of God the Father" (vv. 10-11).

The verses vibrate with power! There is authority in this exalted name that has been given to Jesus. The authority in His name is clearly demonstrated by the fact that someday every knee shall bow before this name and every tongue shall confess that He is Lord.

In his poem "The Golden Legend," Henry Wadsworth Longfellow tells about Friar Pacificus, an old monk, laboring at copying the Scriptures in a medieval scriptorium. When he comes to the name of the Lord Jesus, he writes:

> It is growing dark! Yet one line more,
> And then my work for today is o'er.
> I come again to the name of the Lord!
> Ere I that awful name record,
> That is spoken so lightly among men,
> Let me pause awhile, and wash my pen;
> Pure from blemish and blot must it be,
> When it writes that word of mystery!

I often hear people using God's name in vain. They hurl some bitter invective at someone at whom they are angry, cursing them in the name of God. It is equally common to hear someone use the name "Jesus," "Christ," or "Lord" as a byword.

Don't do it! This exalted name of Jesus is the name above every name. This is the name in which all authority in heaven and on earth rests. Don't do it! This is the holy name before which every knee shall bow some day and which every tongue shall confess as Lord.

We are told in the Scriptures that if we will confess our faith in the name of the Lord Jesus we shall be saved (Rom. 10:9-10). It is clearly taught in Scripture that the day is coming in which everyone shall confess that Jesus is the Lord. Why not then do it today and be saved? If you wait until the judgment to do it, it will be too late and you will forever be lost. But mark it down as a fact: every knee shall bow and every tongue shall confess that Jesus is the Lord as God the Father has said. It is so because of the authority in Jesus' name.

Paul makes it abundantly clear that *every knee* shall bow and *every tongue* shall confess. In verse 10 he says that the knees of all heavenly beings shall bow—angels, cherubim, seraphim, and all the saved in heaven. He also says that every knee on earth shall bow—all those who are still lost when Jesus comes again. All the knees of all beings under the earth shall bow—Satan, demons, and all the fallen angels. Included among these is the Prince of Darkness himself who opposes all the Savior does. This is the authority—the great and matchless authority—which is in the holy name of Jesus.

The Reason the Name Was Given

Why has Jesus been exalted to the Father's right hand and given the name above every name? Verse 11 tells us: "To the glory of God the Father."

Everything created was created for God's glory. Everything Jesus does is done for God's glory. Everything the Holy Spirit does is done for God's glory. Everything the Christian does is to be done for God's glory. The basic, ultimate, and final purpose for everything created is that God might be glorified. The reason that Jesus took on human flesh and was nailed to the cross, raised from the dead, exalted to the Father's right hand, and given the name above every name is that the Heavenly Father might be glorified!

God was glorified in the ancient tabernacle in the wilderness. He was glorified on Mount Sinai when Moses spent forty days there receiving the Ten Commandments (Ex. 24:12-18). When the ark of the covenant was brought into the newly completed temple, the glory of God filled the house (2 Chron. 5:14). The psalmist wrote that the heavens above glorify God (Ps. 19:1). Luke told that when Jesus was born "the glory of the Lord" shone round about the shepherds (Luke 2:9). On that same night, the angelic hosts sang, "Glory to God in the highest and on earth peace, good will toward men" (Luke 2:14, KJV). When Jesus was on the mount of transfiguration, Peter, James, and John saw the glory of God come upon Him (Luke 9:22). When Jesus returns He shall do so on a cloud and coming "with power and great glory" (Luke 21:27).

But the world has never seen the glory of God expressed as it shall be expressed when Jesus comes again, and angels, Satan, demons, the redeemed, the lost, and all creation—animate and inanimate—bow down before him and sing the doxology that he is "King of kings and Lords of lords!" On that day God shall be glorified in everything! This is the reason that the exalted name above every name has been given to Jesus our Lord.

Conclusion

I know of lands that are sunk in shame,
Of hearts that faint and tire:
But I know a Name, a Name, a Name
That can set those lands on fire.

Its sound is a brand, its letters flame
Like glowing tongues of fire.
I know a Name, a Name, a Name
That will set those lands on fire.

—Author unknown

Note

1. R. C. Campbell, *The Christ of the Centuries* (Nashville: Broadman Press, 1947), 7.

7
The Call to Excellence

(Phil. 2:12-24)

Introduction

One of history's greatest musical conductors was Arturo Toscanini. Born in Parma, Italy, in 1867, Toscanini died in his sleep in New York City in 1957. For years he conducted the National Broadcasting Company's Symphony Orchestra in New York City's Carnegie Hall. The last time he conducted there he was eighty-seven years old.

Those who played for Toscanini say he was a terrible taskmaster in rehearsals. Often those rehearsals were battlegrounds between the maestro and his orchestra. He could be ruthless in the verbal tortures he heaped upon some unfortunate musician, but at the same time he could be as gentle as a grandfather.

Once in a rehearsal a member of the orchestra was performing poorly in a solo passage. The white-maned Toscanini rapped his baton for silence. Placing one hand on his hip, he touched the end of his nose with the baton. The orchestra knew from experience that a terrible storm was about to break upon the poor soloist.

An ominous silence filled the room as Toscanini called the player by name. Looking kindly at the trembling musician for a few minutes, Toscanini then asked pleasantly, "Tell me, please, when were you born?"

When the question was answered, the maestro then asked, "And in what month?"

When he learned the month of the man's birth, all wondered what was coming next.

"And on what day of the month were you born?" Toscanini queried.

Now completely unnerved by Toscanini's gentle inquisition, the poor musician answered, "I think it was a Tuesday, Maestro."

Suddenly all of Toscanini's fury was unleashed, and he shouted at the quivering musician, "That was a black day for music!" He then raised his baton in the air, struck the downbeat, and the orchestra began to play as though nothing had happened.

In a moment they arrived at the dreaded solo passage where the small mistake had infuriated Toscanini, but this time the soloist played his part without a bobble.

Stopping the orchestra, the maestro looked at the white-faced soloist and said: "So! So!" With his hand he threw a kiss to the musician he had verbally crucified and then sweetly said: "So you are not stupid. You can play well. Now I am happy. You are happy. Beethoven is happy!"

On another occasion Toscanini was rehearsing his orchestra, and he wanted the piece of music played perfectly. But it was obvious that the orchestra was not giving its best. Laying down his baton, Toscanini said quietly: "Gentlemen, God has told me how he wants this piece of music played and you are hindering God."

Paul had been told of the divisive spirit that has developed in the church at Philippi. The quarrel between Euodia and Syntche (4:2) had affected the church. Paul was unhappy with them. They were unhappy with each other. Jesus was unhappy with their negative attitude. Therefore, Paul wrote to tell them that they were hindering God and to repair the sweet fellowship that once marked the church. God had called them to excellence but they were not conducting themselves on the high plane of love and unselfishness to which they had been called.

Let us look now at these verses and see some of the things that are involved in this holy call to excellence that God has given to each believer in Jesus Christ.

A Call to a New Obedience

Therefore, my dear friends, as you have always obeyed—not only in my presence, but now much more in my absence—continue to work out your salvation with fear and trembling, for it is God who works in you to will and to act according to his good purpose (vv. 12-13).

Paul wanted the Philippians to understand that their obedience to Jesus Christ was a matter of primary importance. Once they were ruled by their sinful nature, but in Christ they had been called to a new obedience.

This new obedience to which the believer is called is clarified in verse 12: "Continue to work out your salvation with fear and trembling."

Lest anyone misunderstand, Paul was not preaching here a gospel of salvation by good works. He clearly refuted that heresy in Ephesians 2:8-10. Rather, he appealed to the Philippians to forsake their self-centered ways (vv. 1-4) and work out in their daily lives what God had worked within them.

God is the divine energizer at work in them and in us. He is the one who "works in you to will and to act according to his good purpose" (v. 13). It is He who has planted within us the seeds of faith and grace that have brought new life. He is at work in us, stirring us up both "to will" and "to act" according to what pleases Him.

This call to excellence to which the Heavenly Father has called us in Jesus Christ is our salvation and all that flows from it. We are to work it out—express it—"with fear and trembling" (v. 12). A. T. Robertson quoted J. B. Lightfoot as saying it means with "a nervous and trembling anxiety to do right."

Paul had no problem here connecting faith and works because he was not telling us how to be saved, but how we are to live after we have been saved. We are to trust in Jesus Christ and him alone as our Savior (Rom. 10:9-10). But after we have been saved, it is our heart's desire to please our Father, and it is He who has put that desire in our hearts. The Holy Spirit within us stirs us up to work out in our lives what God has worked in us through His grace.

American storyteller Archibald Rutledge tells about a man who worked in one of the great forests of the South. His faithful dog had burned to death a few minutes earlier in a great fire that had swept through the forest. Rutledge said the little dog had been left under a tree to guard his master's dinner pail and wouldn't leave it even when the flames roared around him.

The worker was brokenhearted when he found the charred remains of his little friend. With tears streaming down his face, he said: "I always had to be careful what I told him to do, because I knew he would do it."

This, and more, is the kind of obedience to which Christ has called us. The new obedience that is to characterize the believer is based on the obedience of Jesus Himself (v. 8).

A Call to a New Attitude

> Do everything without complaining or arguing, so that you may become blameless and pure, children of God without fault in a crooked and depraved generation, in which you shine like stars in the universe as you hold out the word of life—in order that I may boast on the day of Christ that I did not run or labor for nothing (vv. 14-16).

What is this new attitude that is to mark believers? Robertson summed it up with two statements: "Cheerfulness Under Orders (verse 14)"; and "Perfection in the Midst of Imperfection (verses 15-16a)."[1]

"Do everything without complaining or arguing" (v. 14), is classified by Robertson under "Cheerfulness Under Orders."

Robertson suggested that "The allusion may be to the conduct of Israel in the wilderness (cf. Ex. 16:7ff.; Num. 16:5,10). The Israelites murmured bitterly against Moses and against God repeatedly and with dire results. 'Neither murmur ye, as some of them murmured, and perished by the destroyer" (1 Cor. 10:10)."[2]

In his work on Philippians, Kenneth Wuest wrote that "complaining" ("murmurings"—KJV) translates a word that means, "to mutter, to murmur," and that the pronunciation of the word resembles its meaning. The word was used of the cooing of doves and describes one's murmurings against others rather than against God. It is a subdued type of complaining that indicates the Philippian quarrel had not yet broken out into an open verbal conflict.

"Arguing" ("disputings"—KJV) describes arguments or wrangling. In *The Broadman Bible Commentary* on Philippians, Frank Stagg said that "The church is not to be a gossip club nor a debating society." Each of these words reveals an old attitude that needs to be replaced by a new attitude. This new attitude will express itself in a "blameless and pure" spirit (v. 15).

Paul urged them to quit their "complaining" and "arguing" so that in a wicked world they may be perceived by the world to "become" the kind of sons and daughters of whom God would be pleased (v. 15).

"Blameless" and "pure" refer to character. They have not yet reached that ideal state, but they are to work toward it as God works in them.

To be "blameless" is to live so humbly and carefully that the world cannot find fault with them. To be "pure" is to live a life uncontaminated by the world. Like metal that has been put through the fire and purified, their lives are to be pure "in the midst of a crooked and depraved generation." In a world that lives in darkness because it has turned from the truth, they are to "shine like stars" (v. 15). Christ's call to excellence is a call to live as guiding stars. As the North Star guides the mariner, so the believer is to be a guide to a world that has lost its way. This is done, Paul said, "As you hold out the word of life" (v. 16).

The ideal set forth for the believer by Jesus is perfection: "Be perfect, therefore, as your heavenly Father is perfect" (Matt. 5:48). Someday we shall be perfect, as Jesus is perfect. We have not yet attained that state, but it is to be our goal. To bring us to that goal, the Father is working and we must work (v. 12).

A Call to a New Commitment

Paul had told the Philippians that soon he hoped to send Timothy to bring back word as to how they were doing. There is no one else the apostle could trust with the assignment, for the spiritual welfare of the Philippians is as important to Timothy as it is to Paul. Against this background, Paul says, "For everyone looks out for his own interests, not those of Jesus Christ" (v. 21).

Unfortunately, this sad comment appropriately describes the church today. Most of us are so caught up in looking out for ourselves and our interests that the Lord's work takes a backseat. Is there any wonder then that we are not reaching the world for Christ in our day? To reach our world with the gospel, Christians must heed Christ's call to "seek first his kingdom and his righteousness" (Matt. 6:33). Indeed, this is a call to excellence!

Robertson wrote that Paul brought a very severe indictment against the Roman Christians. Who is included among those who seek their own interests rather than those of Christ we are not told. But of all those who were there in Rome and who could have helped Paul carry his burdens, the most dependable was Timothy. Timothy expressed more concern for Paul's interests, which was in reality a concern for the interests of Jesus, than he did of his own (Matt. 25:41-46).

Timothy's dependability had been proved again and again for "As a son with his father he has served with me in the work of the gospel (v. 22)," Paul declared. "Served" could be translated "slaved." Timothy was as close to Paul as a son, but he had worked with Paul as a slave would work for his master.

This kind of commitment to Jesus has been demonstrated many times in Christian history. Never, however, was it more beautifully demonstrated than in the life of Cambridge University cricket star C. T. Studd, the greatest cricketeer of his day.

In his book *The King and the Kingdom*, William Barclay says that after Studd was saved and called to the mission field, he had the impression that he should dispose of the rather large inheritance his father had left him. He took literally Jesus' words, "Go, sell everything you have and give to the poor" (Mark 10:21).

Studd immediately made out some checks to dispose of his inheritance: 5,000 pounds to D. L. Moody; 5,000 pounds to Salvation Army founder General William Booth; 5,000 pounds to George Muller; 5,000 pounds to Whitechapel Mission; and an additional five checks each for 1,000 pounds. But still Studd had money left over and he tried to give it to his wife but she refused it. Studd sent the remainder of the money to General William Booth and told Booth to say nothing about it to anyone. Studd then wrote in his diary that he could gladly say, "Silver or gold I do not have" (Acts 3:6).

A Call to a New Outlook

Referring to his sending Timothy to the Philippians, Paul wrote in verses 23-24: "I hope, therefore, to send him as soon as I see how things go with me. And I am confident in the Lord that I myself will come soon."

Here is Christian optimism at its best! Timothy would come soon, wrote Paul, but he was also confident that he himself would also come soon.

Robertson pointed out that "The whim of a Nero was an elusive thing to count upon. But he [Paul] no longer thinks of going on to Spain first as he had once planned (Rom. 15:28). His heart now turns to the east (Philem. 22). His long imprisonment in Caesarea and Rome had made it necessary for Paul to set things in order in the east. The Gnostic disturbers already had appeared on the horizon before Paul left Asia (Acts 20:29f.). These 'grievous wolves' had taken full advantage of Paul's absence to play havoc with the flock in various parts of Asia. Philippi also tugs at Paul's heart which now definitely turns eastward. When he was released, it seems probable that he did go east at once. We catch traces of Paul's tracks at Miletus (2 Tim. 4:20), Ephesus (1 Tim. 1:3), Macedonia and so probably Philippi (1 Tim. 1:3), Troas (2 Tim. 4:13), and Nicopolis (Titus 3:12). We may believe, therefore, that in time the Philippians did see Paul again as well as Timothy, who was certainly in the east (1 Tim. 1:3)."[3]

But in spite of all that had happened to Paul, he still had an upbeat, optimistic, faith-filled outlook: "I myself will come soon" (v. 24).

It matters not what cup life presses to the believer's lips—however bitter and distasteful it may be—we must guard against looking at life through dark glasses. God is alive, still on the throne, and ultimately He shall have the victory! That's the new outlook that each of us who is called to excellence must cultivate.

Conclusion

Norman Vincent Peale had a long and distinguished ministry at Marble Collegiate Church in New York City. He preached with confidence and power all over the world, and his messages have been a help to a great many people.

But when Peale first started preaching, his timid nature gave him a lot of problems. When he preached his first sermon at Walpole, Massachusetts, he was so terrified that he wired his father for help.

His preacher father wired back to his young, terrified son: "Prepare your own sermons. Just tell people that Jesus Christ can change their lives. Love, Dad."

It is true. Jesus does change lives, and he has changed many of our lives. He has called us out of darkness into His marvelous light.

This is the word those lost without Jesus need to hear today. Walking in spiritual darkness and groveling in sin, they need to know there is a better way. When once they hear and respond to Christ's call to excellence, their lives will be different!

> To every man there openeth
> A Way, and Ways, and a Way.
> And the High Soul climbs the High Way,
> And the Low Soul gropes the Low,
> And in between, on the misty flats,
> The rest drift to and fro.

But to every man there openeth
A High Way, and a Low.
And every man decideth
The way his soul shall go.
—John Oxenham (1852-1941)

Notes

1. A. T. Robertson, *Paul's Joy in Christ* (Nashville: Broadman Press, 1979), 148-50.
2. Ibid, 148-49.
3. Ibid, 165.

8
Just a Common Christian

(Phil. 2:25-30)

Introduction

A Scottish minister sent his annual report to his church's head-quarters. The report, more of an apology than anything else, went something like this: "I am sorry to tell you that only one person was saved in our church this year, and he was only a boy."

When young Robert Moffatt was saved in that church, probably people thought little about it. He was only a boy—just a common Christian. There was nothing spectacular about him or his conversion. He was such a common, ordinary boy that the pastor half-apologized for the church's failure that year.

But let's take another look at this common Christian. One day Jesus spoke to the boy's heart and called him to missionary service. And, years later, Robert Moffatt opened Africa to the gospel.

After years of service in Africa, Moffatt wrote back to a friend in Scotland that on a clear morning he could see the smoke of a thousand villages where the name of Jesus had never been heard.

Robert Moffatt became a father, and his daughter married David Livingstone. And for more than three decades Livingstone served in Africa as a physician, preacher, and explorer.

Most believers think of themselves only as common, ordinary Christians. If asked what they can do for Jesus, most would reply: "Oh, I can't do very much, for I am just a common Christian. I can't preach. I can't sing. I can't play an instrument. I can't give much money. I can't do much for Jesus. My talents are so meager. I am just a common Christian." But it is these common Christians—just ordinary folk—upon whom Jesus has built His church and who have taken the gospel to the ends of the earth.

In this text we discover a remarkably fine tribute to people who are just ordinary, common Christians. The tribute is from the eminent apostle Paul who was anything but common. He shook empires for Jesus, wrote thirteen books of the New Testament, and preached to kings and other leaders. He was an uncommon Christian in every sense of the word.

Paul's tribute in these verses is directed at Epaphroditus who, perhaps, was a layperson. He never founded a church, never preached a sermon that has been preserved, never wrote a book of the New Testament, and never did any of the things that would mark him out as being an uncommon Christian. He was just a gentle, humble layperson from Philippi whom the church had sent to Rome to see about Paul.

The Philippians had heard that their friend and preacher was in jail, and they were concerned about him. So they sent Epaphroditus from Philippi to Rome with some personal things for their preacher, and they told Epaphroditus to stay there as long as he was needed.

This common Christian is mentioned only two times in the New Testament, and both of those references are in the Book of Philippians.

But Epaphroditus did what he could for Jesus. And because he was faithful and used the talents with which he had been endowed, he is forever memorialized on the pages of the Scriptures.

The tribute the Holy Spirit pays here to Epaphroditus is really an accolade to be laid at the feet of every common, ordinary Christian who does his or her best for Jesus.

Although you may think of yourself as just a common Christian, there are some uncommon things about you.

The Family that Loves You

Epaphroditus is about to return to Philippi and report to the church on Paul's condition. "But I think it is necessary to send back to you Epaphroditus, my brother," Paul wrote (v. 25).

The words, "my brother," identify the special family to which both Epaphroditus and Paul belonged. The word literally means, "from the same womb."

Paul was saying that both he and Epaphroditus are a part of the same family. That family, of course, is the family of God. God is the Father, Jesus is the elder brother, and all the believers are brothers and sisters. It is a special family to which every "common" Christian belongs.

When Paul calls Epaphroditus "my brother," he is saying something very meaningful. Paul was a Jew, and Epaphroditus was a Gentile. For centuries the Jews and the Gentiles had been enemies. The Jews called the Gentiles, "dogs," and the Gentiles returned the compliment. Although Paul was a Jew and Epaphroditus was a Gentile, still they were both "from the same womb." They were brothers in Christ Jesus.

We are not told when Epaphroditus was saved and became a member of this special family. But, perhaps, we can suppose some things and not be too far wrong.

"Epaphroditus" was a pagan name. It means, "devoted to Aphrodite." Aphrodite, or Venus as the Romans called her, was the goddess of love and beauty. It was a pagan religion that reveled in immorality. It is likely that the parents of Epaphroditus were devotees of Aphrodite, and when their little son was born they named him for their pagan goddess.

But something happened to Epaphroditus along the way. Somewhere, perhaps at Philippi, Epaphroditus came under the preaching of the gospel and was saved. Now this Gentile who had been named for a pagan goddess, and this Jew who had been converted on the Damascus Road were members of the same family. They were brothers in Christ.

You may think you are just a common Christian, but don't ever forget that you are a part of a special family.

The Fellowship that Claims You

During World War II, Britons placed large signs at the entrance to their munitions factories. The signs carried only five letters: "IADOM."

A stranger in England during that time probably didn't understand what the signs meant. But the British people knew that the letters were an abbreviation for the words, "It all depends on me." It was a slogan to remind them that they were fighting for their land and lives, that victory depended on them.

Sometimes we Christians act as though the Lord's work depends wholly upon us—individually, that is. Like Elijah, we become discouraged and feel we are the only one in the world who is concerned about the work of God's kingdom.

That's not so. It all doesn't depend upon us. There are millions of Christians who still love Jesus and are serving Him faithfully. There is a special fellowship of which each of us is a part. We are a part of something big and beautiful, and that fellowship encourages and blesses us.

In verse 25 Paul speaks of this special fellowship that all believers share: "But I think it is necessary to send back to you Epaphroditus, my brother, fellow worker and fellow soldier, who is also your messenger, whom you sent to take care of my needs."

Look, especially, at the words "fellow worker" and "fellow soldier." They indicate that more than one person is involved in this fellowship. Epaphroditus was just a common Christian, but he was blessed and strengthened by his fellowship with Paul. On the other hand, Paul was encouraged in his imprisonment by the fellowship of this gentle Gentile who was just a common Christian.

The words "worker" and "soldier," that describe both Paul and Epaphroditus, tell us that their work for Jesus was not easy. It was dangerous and demanding work, even as being a "worker" is demanding and being a "soldier" is dangerous. But their fellowship nerved their hearts.

Being a committed Christian is never easy. It demands the very best that is in us: our best thinking, our best talents, and our best living. Often we must stand against Satan and the world, as a soldier must stand against a charging enemy.

It isn't without cost to be a Christian in the business world, on the campus, or even at home. But there is a special fellowship in our church that strengthens us for life's demands, and we need this fellowship.

The Father that Sustains You

As Epaphroditus prepares to leave Rome for Philippi, Paul sent this letter back describing how sick Epaphroditus has been: "Indeed he was ill, and almost died. But God had mercy on him, and not on him only but also on me, to spare me sorrow upon sorrow" (v. 27).

Paul was talking about the blessed Heavenly Father who sustains all of us. Not only does He sustain his special servants like Paul who serve Him in unique ways, but also he lovingly sustains each of us, who, like Epaphroditus, are just common Christians.

Epaphroditus had been seriously ill, but we are not told what was his problem. Verse 30 tells us that he nearly died, and that his sickness was the result of faithful work for Jesus. Epaphroditus forgot his needs as he poured out his love for Jesus by taking care of Paul. And because of his self-denying life, Epaphroditus had nearly died. Paul is so thankful to God for sparing Epaphroditus that in verse 27 he broke out into a doxology!

All of us can testify to the mercy of God that has been bestowed upon us again and again. We are just common Christians but, still, the Heavenly Father has an uncommon love for us and pours out His mercy upon us without limitation. He is faithful to sustain us and we praise His holy name.

The Future that Awaits You

This is in verse 29. After having been absent for some time, Epaphroditus is returning home to Philippi. Paul is talking about Epaphroditus's future: "Welcome him in the Lord with great joy, and honor men like him."

Epaphroditus was just a common Christian, but Paul told the Philippians to treat Epaphroditus in an uncommon manner upon his arrival home. They were to be good to him and receive him with gladness. They were to give him the honor he justly deserved. He had risked his life for the gospel, and Paul told them to reward the brave missionary accordingly. A very special future awaited Epaphroditus in Philippi. He was just a common Christian, but he was a common Christian with a bright future as he headed home.

But that's exactly what awaits each of us common Christians who is faithful to what Jesus has given us to do. However limited we may feel our abilities are, or however humble we may feel our place of service is, if we serve Jesus faithfully there is a special future that awaits us when we reach home.

Paul talked about this special future that awaits us when he wrote to young Timothy: "Now there is in store for me the crown of righteousness, which the Lord, the righteous Judge, will award to me on that day—and not only to me, but also to all who have longed for his appearing" (2 Tim. 4:8).

Jesus, too, talks about the future that awaits us when He said to His disciples:

> In my Father's house are many rooms; if it were not so, I would have told you. I am going there to prepare a place for you. And if I go and prepare a place for you, I will come back and take you to be with me that you also may be where I am (John 14:2-3).

Conclusion

American evangelist Dwight Moody was mightily used by God. On several occasions he held crusades in England where he was received enthusiastically.

On one of his trips to England, Moody met Henry Varley. Moody's life was forever changed when Varley told him that the world had yet to see what God could do with one who was fully committed to His will.

"Varley," Moody told him, "the words you spoke to me last year at Newcastle about what God could do through one man who was fully committed to Him were sent straight from the living God."

For all his fame and greatness, Moody was just a common Christian who was totally dedicated to Jesus Christ. And as God used Moody, He will use all common Christians who will yield fully to Him.

9
Life's Greatest Treasure

(Phil. 3:1-11)

Introduction

Mel Fisher had a great sixty-fourth birthday.

A treasure hunter, Fisher owned Treasure Salvoras, Inc. and had been looking for the Spanish galleon *Nuestra Senora de Atocha* for seventeen years. The ship, loaded with precious cargo, sank in 1622 during a hurricane. It was on its maiden voyage from Havana to Spain.

On a July day just before his sixty-fourth birthday, Fisher discovered the ship and its treasure about forty miles west of Key West, Florida. Imagine his joy that day as his divers brought up from the deep an estimated 150 pounds of gold, including seventy-six gold bars, gold chains, and gold disks!

In addition to this find, more than nine hundred silver bars and one hundred gold bars have been recovered. It is estimated that the ship's fortune may contain a treasure worth more than $340 million.

Finding a treasure like that is mind-boggling! What red-blooded American has not dreamed of doing the same thing? If he could find a treasure like that, he could make a down payment on his debts and pay the rest off in monthly installments!

But there is a greater treasure waiting to be found. It's neither silver nor gold, and it isn't kept in a bank vault. It doesn't need to be protected from thieves who would come at night and steal it away. It is free and everyone can have it. Multiplied millions of people have found this treasure and claimed it for themselves, but its wealth has not been depleted one iota. There is as much of it today as there ever has been, and everybody can have it.

I am talking about the great treasure of the grace of God that is available to us in Jesus Christ. The New Testament calls it the new birth and salvation.

Life's Greatest Treasure Cannot Be Acquired By Good Works

Paul warned:

> Watch out for those dogs, those men who do evil, those mutilators of the flesh. For it is we who are the circumcision, we who worship by the Spirit of God, who glory in Christ Jesus, and put no confidence in the flesh—though I myself have reason for such confidence (vv. 2-4).

This is a strong warning to the Philippians. It seems to indicate, as A. T. Robertson wrote, that the dissension in the Philippian church had been complicated by Judaizers who insisted that one could only be saved by first submitting to circumcision. Robertson declared that three times Paul made his strong warning to "Beware, beware, beware" of this heresy.[1]

Paul called these false teachers "dogs," but we are not to be too shocked by Paul's hard words. These "dogs," Paul says, are "those men who do evil, those mutilators of the flesh."

"Dogs" was a common word the Gentiles used to refer to the Jews in a derogatory manner. To the Jews, a dog was an unclean animal (Deut. 23:18), a scavenger that roamed the streets and ate what he could find. Paul called these false teachers "spiritual dogs" because they were spiritual scavengers. They worked as hard to make a convert to their heresy as city dogs do to find a scrap of discarded food.

What Paul was rebuking is the heretical doctrine of salvation by grace plus good works. Once and for all he settled that matter for the Ephesians in Ephesians 2:8-10.

Before Martin Luther was saved, he saw God as an angry judge who had passed a sentence of death upon all sinners. Luther longed to be free from the heavy weight of guilt and condemnation that he carried, so he turned to the church and its sacraments.

Hoping to earn the salvation he so desperately wanted, Luther became a monk, fasting often and spending much time in prayer. Frequently, he inflicted physical punishment on his body and went to confession so often that the other monks would hide in embarrassment when they saw Luther coming. He would often spend long hours confessing the most trivial sins. Still he found no peace.

But what Luther could not obtain by his good works, he discovered as he studied the Book of Romans. When he came to Romans 1:17: "As it is written, The just shall live by faith" (KJV), he saw for the first time that salvation was by grace alone and that all his good works were for nothing. Throwing himself fully upon the grace of God, Luther was saved, set free, gave birth to the Protestant Reformation, and sent history reeling in another direction.

Not only is life's greatest treasure not acquired by good works, but also:

Life's Greatest Treasure Cannot Be Earned by Personal Merit

Paul told the Philippians that if anyone could be saved by his merit, he would certainly qualify:

> If anyone else thinks he has reasons to put confidence in the flesh, I have more: circumcised on the eighth day, of the people of Israel, of the tribe of Benjamin, a Hebrew of Hebrews; in regard to the law, a Pharisee; as for zeal, persecuting the church; as for legalistic righteousness, faultless (vv. 4-6).

Paul recounted here his personal merits that surely would have qualified him to receive the grace of God if grace came through merit. But it did not as he clearly pointed out.

He was "circumcised on the eighth day, of the people of Israel." Male Gentile converts to Judaism were circumcised in maturity, Ishmaelites in the thirteenth year, and Jews on the eighth day (Gen. 17:12; Luke 2:21).

Paul was no Jewish proselyte. He was pure Israelite "of the stock of Israel," as the *King James Version* puts it. He came from the "original stock of Jacob whose covenant name was Israel (Gen. 32:28)," Robertson wrote in *Paul's Joy in Christ*.

Continuing to stack higher his list of personal merits that would have qualified him for the grace of God if it could be acquired by merit, Paul added: "Of the tribe of Benjamin, a Hebrew of Hebrews."

Benjamin was the son of Rachel, Jacob's beloved wife. He was the only son of Jacob born in Palestine. The tribe gave Israel Saul, its first king. Benjamin was the most honored tribe in battle. Benjamin alone remained faithful to Judah when the kingdom was divided (1 Kings 12:21). After the exile Benjamin merged with Judah (Ezra 4:1). Paul was proud of his heritage—as a descendant of Benjamin.

Paul was also "a Hebrew of Hebrews." In *Word Pictures in the New Testament*, A. T. Robertson explains that Paul came from Hebrew parents who had retained the "characteristic qualities in language and custom" as distinct from the Hellenistic, or Greek-speaking Jews. Paul knew Greek, Aramaic, and Hebrew, but he had not forsaken the Hebrew language and customs of his people for those of the Greeks. He was fiercely proud of his heritage.

The personal merits that have been listed by Paul to this point had come to him through his heritage. The things that now follow are of his own choosing: Pharisee, zealous persecutor of the church, and strict observer of the Mosiac law.

Paul's father was a Pharisee (Acts 23:6). Paul had studied in Jerusalem under Gamaliel, one of Israel's finest (22:3). As a Pharisee, Paul highly revered and strictly obeyed the laws of Moses. His zeal for protecting that law drove him to become a persecutor of the church. He was among those persecutors who slew Stephen (7:59 to 8:1). Before Paul was saved, he was the persecutor, but after he was saved he was the persecuted. Concerning his adherence to the law of Moses, he was "faultless." Robertson said that Paul "knew and practiced all the rules of the Rabbis. A marvelous record, scoring a hundred in Judaism."

But after having listed all his personal merits, Paul quickly points out that none of these brought to him the grace of God in Jesus Christ. So far as salvation was concerned, they were worthless.

A final thing needs to be said about life's greatest treasure:

Life's Greatest Treasure Is Worth Any Cost

"But whatever was to my profit I now consider loss for the sake of Christ. What is more, I consider everything a loss compared to the surpassing greatness of knowing Christ Jesus my Lord" (vv. 7-8).

Once Paul counted his heritage and merits, as Robertson wrote, like a miser listening to "the clink of every piece of gold." But he had been changed. His values were different. He found something of such infinite value that he was willing to pay any price required to have it.

Paul's personal ledger of "assets" and "liabilities" has also been changed. The things which he once added up in his ledger with plus signs now have minus signs by them. And the things he once put in the minus column have been shifted to the plus column.

"What is more," Paul continued, is that he now considered "everything a loss compared to the surpassing greatness of knowing Christ Jesus my Lord" (v. 8).

These introductory words of verse 8, "What is more," are, according to Kenneth Wuest, five particles which literally could be translated, "yea, indeed, therefore, at last, even!" Driven by his consuming passion for Jesus, Paul piled these articles on top of each other as his words seem to run together. At the outset of his Christian life Paul considered "everything a loss" for Christ. And the use of the present tense indicates his attitude had not changed. He still believed, long years after he had been saved, that what he traded for what he got was well worth the cost!

The "surpassing greatness of knowing Christ" (v. 8) is, to Paul, life's greatest treasure. Compared to all he learned about God from Gamaliel and others, Paul's knowledge of Christ was of "surpassing greatness." He looked back over his experience with Christ and confesses joyously that it had been worth everything he paid to acquire it.

As though he had not dwelt sufficiently on the value of what he had acquired in Christ, contrasted to what he was before he met Jesus, Paul added:

> I consider them rubbish, that I may gain Christ and be found in him, not having a righteousness of my own that comes from the law, but that which is through faith in Christ—the righteousness that comes from God and is by faith. I want to know Christ and the power of his resurrection and the fellowship of sharing in his sufferings, becoming like him in his death, and so, somehow, to attain to the resurrection from the dead (vv. 8-11).

Paul had surrendered his self-righteousness for "the righteousness that comes from God and is by faith" (v. 9). Frank Stagg said this righteousness is to be understood as a synonym for salvation. "God accepts the sinner with a view to making him righteous. 'Righteousness' is not only a new relationship with God; it is also a new kind of existence, a new quality of life—of attitude and action—rightness within one's life and in his conduct. It is the triumph of good over evil, not as man's doing but of God's work."[2]

In all he did, Paul wanted "to know Christ and the power of his resurrection" (v. 10). Neither the historical resurrection of Jesus nor Paul's own resurrection is the emphasis here. Rather, Paul wanted to experience in his life the quality of spiritual power that brought Jesus Christ back from the dead (Rom. 6:4-11).

But Paul also aspires "to attain to the resurrection from the dead" (v. 11). The once-proud Paul described in verses 4-6 is no more. Here is the humble, saved Paul devoutly confident that he too would be raised from the dead.

He has eloquently told us in these verses that the greatest treasure of life is to know Christ. This treasure is of supreme value. It is worth whatever it may cost us. Paul knows nothing that is more desirable or valuable than this. For him, and for us, having Jesus is life's greatest treasure.

Conclusion

Many of us have read the novel *Ben Hur* or we have seen the 1959 movie version.

It is the thrilling story of Judah Ben-Hur and his conversion to Christianity. One of the most moving scenes of the movie is the crucifixion of Christ on Calvary.

The author of *Ben Hur* was politician Lew Wallace (1827-1905). The man who challenged Wallace to write *Ben Hur* was Robert Ingersoll (1833-1899). Neither Wallace nor Ingersoll was a Christian. Ingersoll was a lawyer and an agnostic who over a thirty-year period attacked Christianity at every opportunity.

One day Ingersoll and Wallace were riding together on a train when Ingersoll challenged Wallace, who was also a capable writer, to write a novel on the life of Christ. Ingersoll's suggestion was that an interesting novel could be written on the moral character of Jesus. "It will be a best-seller," Ingersoll told Wallace.

Wallace accepted Ingersoll's challenge and during the time he was governor of the New Mexico Territory, Wallace wrote *Ben Hur*.

But a strange thing happened as Wallace wrote his novel. In studying the life of Jesus from the Gospels, Wallace was saved!

It has happened again and again through history. When a sinner takes seriously the claims of Jesus Christ as they are presented in the Gospels, he is transformed as he discovers life's greatest treasure.

Well did the poet describe life's greatest treasure when he wrote:

> I've tried in vain a thousand ways,
> My fears to quell, my hopes to raise;
> And all I need, the Bible says
> Is Jesus.
>
> My soul is night, my heart is steel,
> I cannot see, I cannot feel;
> For light, for life I must appeal
> To Jesus.

He dies, He lives, He reigns, He pleads,
There's love in all His words and deeds;
All, all a guilty sinner needs
Is Jesus.

Though some will mock, and some will blame,
In spite of fear, in spite of shame,
I'll go to Him, because His name
Is Jesus.[3]

—Author unknown

Notes

1. A. T. Robertson, *Paul's Joy in Christ* (Nashville: Broadman Press, 1979), 176.

2. Frank Stagg, *The Broadman Bible Commentary*, Vol. 11, "2 Corinthians-Philemon" (Nashville: Broadman Press), 207.

3. George W. Truett, *Follow Thou Me* (Nashville: Broadman Press, 1932), 144.

10
Made for the High Places

(Phil. 3:12-14)

Introduction

The nineteenth-century Danish philosopher and Protestant theologian Sören Kierkegaard gives a powerful lesson in a story about some wild geese.

The geese came and went with the seasons as their ancestors had done for centuries. One day some of the geese, on their annual trek, landed in a farmer's barnyard. He adopted them and saw to it that they had plenty of grain to eat. Life was easy and the geese decided they had found a fine place to live out the rest of their days.

But as time went along the easy life took its toll. The geese became fat and lazy, and their ambition to soar again in the high places waned. When they heard the familiar honks of their friends high above, the fat, lazy, barnyard geese could only casually look up.

Occasionally, one of them would have an old stirring deep inside to join his friends and soar again where the air was pure, sweet and bracing. One day those stirrings were too strong for one of the geese to resist, and it started its courageous run across the pasture, extended its wings, became airborne for only a few feet, and then plopped not-too-gracefully back to terra firma!

Before long the call to the high places all but vanished in the barnyard geese. Their friends would fly over, honking their call to the higher, nobler life, but the grounded geese paid little attention as they contentedly pecked away at the farmer's corn. And soon the desire to return to the sky and the long flights to freedom disappeared altogether.

They were made for the high places, but the soft life had ruined them.

In this Scripture passage we are considering, Paul is telling us that we, too, were made for the spiritual high places. Epaphroditus has come from Philippi to Rome, where Paul was a prisoner, with the news that the Philippian church was not doing too well. Pride had invaded the church and some of the believers, pursuing their self-centered ways, were living in the low, spiritual swamp of pride where the air was heavy and foul. The once-pure fellowship of the Philippian church had been poisoned by the noxious fumes of self-ishness.

Paul wrote to tell them that God made them for better things, and that they were to press on with holy determination to Christlikeness of character. Theirs is a divine call to the higher life.

The same thing is true for us today. We can take the high road or the low road. We can live in the foul swamp of self-centeredness or reach for the high places of spiritual maturity. The choice is ours.

John Oxenham wrote this about the choice:

> To every man there openeth
> A Way, and Ways, and a Way.
> The High Soul climbs the High Way,
> And the Low Soul gropes the Low,
> And in between, on the misty flats,
> The rest drift to and fro.
> But to every man there openeth
> A High Way, and a Low.
> And every man decideth
> The Way his soul shall go.

For us Christians who would live on the high plane of spiritual maturity and Christlikeness, there are some encouragements given in these verses.

The Person Who Encourages Us

The one who encourages us in our quest for the nobler life is identified in verse 12: "Not that I have already obtained all this, or have already been made perfect, but I press on to take hold of that for which Christ Jesus took hold of me."

Elizabeth Barrett Browning, one of Great Britain's best-known poets and the author of *Sonnets from the Portuguese,* was once asked to account for her success. Mrs. Browning simply replied: "I had a friend."

She was talking about her husband, Robert Browning. When they married, Elizabeth was almost a permanent invalid. She thought she would spend the rest of her life on her couch, as she put it. But after she fell in love with Browning, things changed. His great love for her literally lifted Elizabeth off her sickbed.

She had written some love sonnets—expressions of her love for Browning—and since she was rather dark-skinned, as one from Portugal might be, Browning suggested she call them "Sonnets from the Portuguese."

The secret behind her success was a friend, she said.

Paul was talking here about his friend Jesus. "He is the one encouraging me to take the high road and live the noble life," Paul proclaimed.

The apostle is looking back at his conversion on the road to Damascus. It was there that Jesus "took hold" of him. The words literally mean, to seize, to catch, to take possession of, to lay hold of as to make a thing one's own. The grammar shows that Jesus took hold of Paul decisively and deliberately, and that the Savior's grip was permanent! Paul's conversion was so powerful that he was never able to get away from its call to high and noble living.

Norman Vincent Peale told in his book *The Amazing Results of Positive Thinking,* that Henry Ford and a friend were lunching together one day when the friend surprised Ford with the question, "Who is your best friend?"

The man then named several people, but Ford didn't respond. Then, taking a pencil, Ford wrote on the tablecloth: "Your best friend is he who brings out the best that is within you."

That's the kind of friend Jesus is. He brings out the best that is in us. He encourages us to be our best and do our best. His encouragement to the higher life is seen throughout the Gospels. His common greeting to His disciples was, "Be of good cheer!" His common message to His disciples was, "Blessed are ye! Blessed are ye!" And His common benediction to His disciples was, "Peace I leave with you!"

Jesus is our encouraging friend who never fails us. And we desperately need a friend like Jesus, for he always points us upward toward life's high places for which we were made.

Second, in this upward call to excellence we must remember:

The Prize Which Awaits Us

Paul talked about the prize that awaits us in verse 14: "I press on toward the goal to win the prize for which God has called me heavenward in Christ Jesus."

What was Paul talking about? What is the prize? In verse 12, he confessed that he has not yet obtained it. But he added that he has been "caught hold of" by Jesus in order to gain it. He says in verse 14 that he is "pressing on toward the goal" that Jesus has set before him.

What does he mean? What is this special prize that the Savior had set before Paul and before each of us?

It is Christlikeness in character. That was the ultimate goal Jesus set before us when He saved us. That final, glorious thing toward which the Father is working in redemption is to develop within us the character of Jesus Christ. The Father's heart is set upon this above all else, for by it His name will be glorified. This is the "prize of the high calling of God in Christ Jesus," as the *King James Version* translates it. And this is the "good" for which God is working all things for those who love Him (Rom. 8:28).

You see, Jesus has not saved us just to keep us out of hell or to get us to heaven. Without question, these are basic reasons for the death, burial, and resurrection of Jesus. But they are not the only reasons.

There is more, much more. More than anything in heaven on earth, God the Father desires for us to become like his dear son Jesus

Christ: "Dear friends, now we are children of God. . . . But we know that when he appears, we shall be like him, for we shall see him as he is" (1 John 3:2). From this eternal goal which the Father has set for us, he will not be deterred!

Soon the day is coming when we shall stand before the Father in heaven. Close by will be our Savior and Elder Brother, the Lord Jesus. On that day, the Father will look at His only begotten Son and then at His sons and daughters by grace, and be able to say to Himself: "Ah, it was worth all it cost. Look! They all have the family likeness" (Rom. 8:29-30; 1 Cor. 15:49).

There is a children's story about an ugly, little duckling who didn't know who or what he was. It caused him a great deal of pain, and his self-esteem was very low.

He was a misfit. He didn't look like the other ducks, and his mother was so ashamed of him that she drove him away. Neither the ducks nor the chickens would have anything to do with him, and he couldn't keep up with the geese. He came to the conclusion that he was neither duck, chicken, nor goose.

But one day the ugly, little fellow found himself. As he watched some beautiful fluffy creatures float across the pond, he was so impressed that he moved up for a closer look. Then it happened! He looked down in the water and saw himself, and to his amazement he discovered that he looked just like the beautiful swans that were swimming nearby.

Is the point not obvious? We may not feel we are making much progress in our Christian walk, but daily God is conforming us to the image of His precious Son. Someday we shall stand by the side of Jesus and, perchance, we will look down into the water of the river of life that flows by the Father's throne and see that we look like Jesus!

That glorious change is sure to happen. Nothing will hinder it. The Father's heart has been fixed on that one thing from before eternity. That's why God saved us! For all eternity He will be surrounded by His sons and daughters of grace, and they will all have the family likeness.

The Price Which Is Demanded of Us

Most of the things in life that are worth having don't come easily. Paul tells us here that there is a price we must pay if we are to move from the spiritual lowlands to the spiritual high places: "But one thing I do: Forgetting what is behind and straining toward what is ahead, I press on toward the goal to win the prize for which God has called me heavenward in Christ Jesus" (vv. 13-14).

The apostle used some strong words to show us the price that must be paid to reach the goal God has set before us. But knowing the thing for which we were created and redeemed, makes paying the price worth it.

When Paul writes in verse 13 of "straining toward what is ahead," he describes a runner. At the end of the track upon which he ran was the prize to be given to the winner. That prize was usually a wreath to crown the winner. To merit the crown, the runner had to struggle toward the goal with all his might. There were strong competitors vying for the prize, but only the one who paid the price and won the race would receive it.

Paul declared, in verse 13, that to win this glorious prize at the end of life's race some things must be forgotten. No doubt he was referring to those things listed in verses 5 and 6 that once were so important to him: an Israelite from the tribe of Benjamin that gave Israel its first king; from solid, respectable Hebrew stock; one of the ruling Pharisees, zealous in his service to God; and committed to keeping the Commandments given by Moses.

But when Paul was claimed by Jesus for Himself on the Damascus road, He gave Paul a new set of values and Paul laid aside the things in which he once gloried. In order to have Christ, Paul had to forget the things in which he gloried and lay aside everything that hindered him.

In verse 13 he says he is "straining toward what is ahead." He was leaning forward toward the goal. As A. T. Robertson put it, "He is on the home stretch." All his energies, like those of a runner, were focused on the goal. He was pressing on, straining toward the goal at the end of the race (v. 14).

To be like Jesus is life's "Holy Grail." It is to be sought and treasured above all things. The matter of Paul's affection and allegiance was forever settled: "One thing I do," he exclaimed (v. 13). Christlikeness is the prize. Commitment and abandonment to Jesus, and Jesus alone, is the price. Paul was determined to pay it.

Everything we want has a price tag on it. Every sin carries a price tag. But the Heavenly Father has set a prize before us worthier, nobler, and more desirable than anything that can be imagined. He wants to make us like Jesus, and the Father has paid a great price to do it. And we must pay a price, too. It will cost us everything, but it is worth everything.

This is the thing for which we were made. This is the thing for which we were redeemed by the precious blood of Jesus. We are not tadpoles made to swim in muddy sloughs. No! We are eagles made to soar where the challenges are great and the spiritual air is rare and pure. We were made for the high places, and the price is worth the prize!

Conclusion

E. Stanley Jones told about a robin that was offered a worm for a feather. *It is a good bargain,* thought the robin. *I won't miss one feather, and it will save me a lot of pecking in hard ground.* So he paid the price for the delicious prize.

The next day he was offered another worm for another feather, and he made the trade. And the next day the same thing happened. The trading feathers for worms continued until one day the robin stretched out his bare wings to fly and found he was earthbound.

God had made the robin to fly, but he would never again soar above the trees of the forest. He had paid too much for too little.

It's a good lesson to remember. God has made us for Himself. He saved us in order to make us like Jesus. The spiritual high places—character, joy, peace, fellowship with our Lord—are ours for the taking. But as Ella Wheeler Wilcox put it, the choice of what we do about it is up to us.

> One ship drives east and another drives west
> With the selfsame winds that blow.
> 'Tis the set of the sails
> And not the gales
> Which tells us the way to go.
>
> Like the winds of the sea are the ways of fate,
> As we voyage along through life:
> 'Tis the set of a soul
> That decides its goal,
> And not the calm or the strife.
>   —Ella Wheeler Wilcox (1855-1919)

11
Blessed Certainties

(Phil. 3:20-21)

Introduction

Lloyd Douglas, the author of *The Robe*, wrote about a violin teacher who had a studio in a building that housed other studios. Occasionally, Douglas would stop by the studio to visit his friend.

"And what's the good news for today?" Douglas asked cheerily one morning when he stopped by to see his friend.

The musician picked up a tuning fork and struck it with a padded mallet. As the melodious sounds filled the studio, the violinist said: "The good news today is, that is 'A.'

"The soprano down the hall misses her high notes and the piano across the hall is off-key. But, my friend, that sound you hear from my tuning fork is 'A.'

"It was 'A' yesterday. It is 'A' today. It will be 'A' tomorrow. It will never change. The good news is, that is 'A.'"[1]

The violinist meant that he had found something that was certain, dependable, and unchanging in a changing and uncertain world.

In this text Paul was talking about some certainties that do not change. From Rome where he was a prisoner, he wrote to his beloved friends at Philippi to assure them that although they lived in a world that was constantly changing, there are some spiritual things that never change.

Here are three blessed certainties that Paul shares with the Philippians to encourage them in their Christian lives.

The Certainty of a Heavenly Home

Paul painted a dark picture of the unsaved in verses 18 and 19. He said they were "enemies of the cross of Christ," "their destiny is destruction," "their God is their stomach," "their glory is in their shame," and "their mind is on earthly things."

Against this black background, Paul described the Christian as one whose "citizenship is in heaven" (v. 20). He then declared two things about our heavenly home.

It Is a Personal Home

Paul spoke about "our" citizenship. He has said that the unsaved person's "destiny is destruction" (v. 19), but now he has a personal word for the believer.

Although these humble believers lived at Philippi in Macedonia, far from the capital city of Rome, still they were Roman citizens for Philippi was a Roman colony. Their names were on the Roman roll. Each was a citizen. No one was excluded. Their citizenship was a personal thing.

Paul is telling us that we Christians are citizens of two worlds. Our name is on the state roll and the national roll, but we have another citizenship that is much more important. We are citizens of the heavenly king. It is personal. Of each of us it is said that "our" citizenship is in heaven. Heaven is our home.

It Is a Permanent Home

"Our citizenship is in heaven" (v. 20). Look now at the little two-letter verb "is."

The grammar in the Greek indicates that something took place in the past, and the condition extends unchanged into the present and the future.

Our name was written in the Lamb's Book of Life on the day we trusted in Christ as our Savior (Rev. 21:27), and it is still written there. Our heavenly citizenship is permanent. It is secure. It is certain.

This verb also appears in 2:6 where it describes Christ's eternal deity: "'Being' in very nature God." He is God and always will be God. That won't change, and neither will our heavenly citizenship. It is as secure, dependable, and certain as is the deity of Jesus Christ.

Thus, by the use of one small, two-letter verb the Holy Spirit assures us that we need not worry about losing our heavenly citizenship. It is permanently fixed.

The late George W. Truett, who was pastor of the First Baptist Church of Dallas, Texas, for forty-seven years, told in his sermon, "The Door to Heaven," about an army surgeon who was riding across the battlefield at Gettysburg after that terrible battle. He was looking carefully at fallen soldiers, checking for any signs of life. As he came to a trench and looked down upon a soldier lying there upon his back, the surgeon thought to himself, *I am too late. He is already gone.*

But even as he was thinking it was too late for him to help, he saw a faint smile on the lips of the wounded soldier. Dismounting, the surgeon knelt down and put his ear to the lips of the soldier and heard him whisper: "Here!" "Here!" "Here!"

Gently shaking the soldier awake, the surgeon asked, "Why were you saying 'Here'?"

Very faintly the dying soldier replied: "They were calling the roll in heaven and I was answering to my name."

It won't be long now. Soon the roll will be called up yonder. If we are trusting in Jesus as our Savior, when our name is called we will be able to answer "Here." It is one of the blessed certainties of which Jesus assures us.

The Certainty of a Returning Redeemer

"And we eagerly await a Savior from there [heaven], the Lord Jesus Christ" (v. 20).

Occasionally, the Roman emperor would visit the outlying colonies. His coming was the most exciting event a Roman citizen could imagine. All kinds of preparations would be made to be sure the emperor had a proper welcome.

Paul used an analogy with which his readers would easily identify. As the emperor would occasionally come, so Jesus, our glorious and heavenly Emperor, will most certainly come for His people.

There are two things to notice here about the returning Redeemer.

The One Who Is Coming

The verse uses the royal, regal names and titles of the One who is coming: "Savior," "Lord," "Jesus," and "Christ."

The One who is coming is the "Savior," the One who redeemed us from our sins (Luke 2:11). He is "Jesus," the son of Mary, so named by the angel (Matt. 1:20-21). He is the "Christ," the promised Messiah of the Jews (Acts 2:36). He is the "Lord," the name most used by the disciples of Jesus after His resurrection (John 20:18).

The Attitude Toward His Coming

"We eagerly await a Savior" (v. 20). The words "eagerly await" describe an attitude of intense yearning, of eager anticipation.

As the Roman citizens in the colonies would eagerly await the coming of their emperor, being certain everything was ready for his coming, so we Christians should stand on our tiptoes, as it were, joyously anticipating His coming. To "eagerly await" Him is to be spiritually and morally prepared to meet Him.

I saw this kind of joyous anticipation graphically pictured some years ago as I was flying from the West Coast back to my home in Texas. It was night and near me sat a chaplain returning from Vietnam who had not seen his family for many months.

As the lights of El Paso appeared in the distance he pressed against the window and stared out into the inky darkness, looking longingly into the night. When we landed, the chaplain's beautiful wife and two small children came running toward him with their arms extended. Then they met, fell into each other's arms, and had a joyful reunion.

This is the kind of anticipation that must fill our hearts as we eagerly await the coming of our Lord and Savior Jesus Christ.

The Certainty of a Blessed Body

"Who, by the power that enables him to bring everything under his control, will transform our lowly bodies so that they will be like his glorious body" (v. 21).

The Kind of Body We Have Today

Paul describes our natural, human body as "lowly." He is not talking about the material out of which we are made: "For he knows how we are formed, he remembers that we are dust" (Ps. 103:14). Rather, he is describing what our body has become as a result of sin. It is "lowly" as the *New International Version* translates it, or "vile" as the *King James Version* puts it.

The bodies God gave Adam and Eve functioned perfectly. But then Adam and Eve fell from their high, sinless state by their own choice, and the debilitating power of sin went to work in their bodies. The result is that our bodies have been brought "low." The word appears in ancient secular Greek literature to describe the Nile River at its drought stage. All of us suffer in our bodies because of sin. Some of that sin is of our own doing and some of it is the doing of others, but sin has brought our bodies "low."

Rejoice now in:

The Kind of Body We Shall Have Tomorrow

Jesus "will transform our lowly bodies so they will be like unto his glorious body" (v. 21).

The scene changes. Paul now describes the sudden, instantaneous, once-for-all change these bodies shall undergo at the coming of Jesus. Although our bodies have been overcome and brought down by sin that has produced disease and death, the Heavenly Father will give us the victory. Our heavenly bodies will overcome disease and triumph over death. They will become immortal, never again subject to disease or death (1 Cor. 15). The grammar used by Paul promises a sudden, victorious, permanent glorification of our bodies.

What will our transformed, glorious and heavenly body be like? Paul answers: "Like his glorious body" (v. 21).

He clarifies this for us in 1 Corinthians 15:49: "And just as we have borne the likeness of the earthly man [Adam], so shall we bear the likeness of the man from heaven."

And what kind of resurrection body did Jesus have? In his book *The Life Beyond*, Ray Summers describes it: It was visible and tangible (Mark 16:14; John 20:18; 1 Cor. 9:1, etc.) Mary Magdalene touched His body (Matt. 28:9), and Thomas was invited to do so (John 20:27). It was a real body (Luke 24:42-43); Matt. 28:9; et al).

It was transcendent. Unlike the resuscitation to life of Lazarus, the son of the widow of Nain, and Jarius's daughter—all of whom died again—Jesus' resurrection was not "a restoration to the natural plane of life."[2]

It was neither subject to time nor space. Jesus appeared to His disciples in a room with locked doors and windows (John 20:19-26). Breaking bread with the two disciples of Emmaus, Jesus suddenly vanished (Luke 24:31).

Other things could be said about Jesus' resurrected body that shall be the pattern for our new bodies. Suffice it to say that "Now we are children of God, and what we will be has not yet been made known. But we know that when he appears, we shall be like him, for we shall see him as he is" (1 John 3:2).

And how is Jesus going to accomplish this stupendous feat of transforming our bodies? Paul answered: "By the power that enables him to bring everything under his control" (v. 21).

It is military language. As a general gives the command and his soldiers arrange themselves quickly before him for inspection, so Jesus will give the command at His coming and all things shall immediately be brought under His divine lordship and rule.

Conclusion

Some say that Arturo Toscanini was the greatest musical conductor of all time. He was the conductor of both the Metropolitan

Opera in New York City and the National Broadcasting Company's Symphony Orchestra.

One day after Toscanini had put his orchestra through a rigorous rehearsal of Beethoven's *Fifth Symphony,* the second violinist leaned over and said to the first violinist: "If the old man scolds us after that, I think I'll push him off the platform."

But Toscanini didn't scold. With his long, white mane falling down across his shoulders, the old maestro extended his arms and opened them as though he would embrace the orchestra. Then, speaking just above a whisper, Toscanini said: "Who am I? Who are you? I am nobody. You are nobody. But Beethoven? Ah, Beethoven is everything."

That's what Paul thought about Jesus. And that's what every believer from Philippi to your town in the twentieth century should think about his or her Savior who has given to us these blessed certainties.

Indeed, Jesus is everything!

Notes

1. J. B. Fowler, *Living Illustrations from History, Literature, and Life* (Nashville: Broadman Press, 1985), 21.

2. Ray Summers, *The Life Beyond* (Nashville: Broadman Press, 1959), 45-46 (quoted).

12
The Bruised Bride

(Phil. 4:1-9)

Introduction

Most church controversies are over matters of little importance, it seems. Probably few churches are divided over doctrinal heresy.

For example, Benjamin P. Browne tells about a wealthy man in New England who built a beautiful colonial church building as a family memorial. Everything about the building was as fine as could be, including the kitchen.

After the church was dedicated, some of the good women decided they wanted to add an electric potato peeler to the kitchen equipment. The device would wash, scrub, and peel potatoes in much less time than doing it by hand required.

But there were some other women who objected to the newfangled gadget. They had been peeling potatoes the old way for years, enjoying many hours of pleasant gossip as they worked. They saw the modern gadget as a threat to their long-held tradition.

Partisan groups soon developed throughout the church. One group was determined to have the new potato peeler, and the other group was determined there would be no new potato peeler in their beautiful kitchen. Soon the husbands were involved, and before long "the entire church membership was divided," as Browne says, "into the pro-potato parer party and the anti-potato parer party."[1]

The pastor of the church became greatly depressed over the situation that had developed. The church had been a pleasant pastorate, but the potato-peeler controversy had torn the fellowship so that he was on the verge of resigning.

When Browne asked the pastor why he would consider giving up such a fine church, the pastor replied: "When I get up to preach on Sunday morning, there before me are the two parties bristling with belligerency—the pro-potato parer party and the anti-potato parer party. Utterly absurd as it seems, their minds are concentrated on this quarrel so that I cannot get through to them with any spiritual message. The potato parer is 'all in all' to them. It has cut my church sharply in two, and I give up because I can no longer preach the gospel and be heard in such an atmosphere."[2]

When Epaphroditus visited Paul during his first imprisonment in Rome, Epaphroditus brought word to the apostle that the Philippian church was having some problems. (2:14; 4:2f) The once-sweet fellowship was strained. Feelings were hurt. People were angry with each other. The disunity of the church was not yet critical but it was threatened, and Paul wanted to make sure things didn't get worse (1:27; 2:1-4; 4:1-9).

Although the problem wasn't over how to peel potatoes, it could have been over something just as absurd. We are not told what the problem was, but we know that the sweet bride of Jesus at Philippi was bruised by the attitude of two women, Euodia and Syntyche, and Paul wrote urging these women to lay aside their differences.

As we look at this text, there are three things I want to show you about Christ's bruised bride at Philippi.

The Problems in the Church

> I plead with Euodia and I plead with Syntyche to agree with each other in the Lord. Yes, and I ask you, loyal yokefellow, help those women who have contended at my side in the cause of the gospel, along with Clement and the rest of my fellow workers, whose names are in the book of life (vv. 2-3).

Two faithful women in the church were quarreling and, apparently, it had begun to affect the whole church. What may have started as a personal squabble between these women, now had the potential of dividing the fellowship of the church Paul had established.

Bruised a Sweet Fellowship

Paul refers to the church as those "whom I love and long for, my joy and crown" (v. 1).

The church at Philippi had always been a delight to Paul. On his second missionary journey, Paul had stopped at Philippi. There he had preached his first sermon on the continent of Europe. During his brief stay, he founded a church (Acts·16).

Whereas the church at Corinth was a constant concern to Paul, the church at Philippi was a constant joy and a source of refreshing to the apostle. Paul and the believers enjoyed a close relationship which was demonstrated by their continuing concern for Paul. They have sent Epaphroditus to Rome to check on Paul's condition, and Epaphroditus had brought some love gifts to Paul from the Philippians. Indeed, they were the apostle's "joy and crown." But now, with the quarrel of Euodia and Syntyche having spilled over into the church, the sweet fellowship had been bruised.

Brought by Two Women

Paul was told by Epaphroditus about Euodia and Syntyche's attitude toward each other. Their problem was of a personal nature, but as is often the case personal problems between church members often become churchwide problems.

Paul knows these are strong-willed women, and he will show no favoritism: "I plead with Euodia and I plead with Syntyche." He pleads with each of them so that neither will think he is blaming either of them for the problem. He pleads with them "to agree with each other in the Lord" (v. 2). They have a personal problem, but they also have a common basis upon which to resolve their problem for each is "in the Lord."

Blackened a Great Heritage

The great heritage of the Philippian church is hinted at in Paul's words of verse 3: "Help these women who have contended at my side in the cause of the gospel, along with Clement and the rest of my fellow workers whose names are in the book of life."

It is obvious from what Paul wrote here that the Philippian church had been aggressive in spreading the gospel in Macedonia. Those devout believers named "had contended" at Paul's side "in the cause of the gospel." So, the heritage of the church was one of strong, evangelistic witnessing to a pagan world. But the problem between Euodia and Syntyche now had been swept into the church, and this great heritage of a mission-minded church has been blackened by the quarrel.

An unknown writer asked the question, "What makes a church great?" Here is his answer:

> Not soft seats and subdued light,
> But strong, courageous leadership.
> Not the sweet tones of the organ,
> But sweet personalities that,
> Somehow reflect Jesus.
> Not the tall towers with chimes and bells,
> But a lofty vision of its people.
> Not big budgets,
> But big hearts.
>
> Not the amount of finance received,
> But the amount of service rendered.
> Not the large membership,
> But God's presence and direction in power.
> Not what it has done in the past,
> But what it is doing now,
> And will do tomorrow.

These are the very things that the church stood to lose. Its leadership had been strong and courageous, but now it is quarreling and divided. The lives of the people had reflected Jesus, but now they are quarreling and that divine reflection has begun to dim. The church had a lofty vision of reaching Macedonia, but now the schism had taken the front seat. Big hearts had beat there, but now smallness of spirit threatens the fellowship. The church had rendered sacrificial service, but now that service is endangered. God's presence, direction, and power had been felt there, but now the church's spiritual power is being drained off on matters that didn't matter.

Having dealt with the problems in the church, Paul moved on to describe the:

Peace for the Church

> Rejoice in the Lord always. I will say it again: Rejoice! Let your gentleness be evident to all. The Lord is near. Do not be anxious about anything, but in everything by prayer and petition, with thanksgiving, present your requests to God. And the peace of God, which transcends all understanding will guard your hearts and your minds in Christ Jesus (vv. 4-6).

Paul came to the defense of the bruised bride of Jesus. Peace must return to the fellowship. The bride must be treated lovingly. Thus, Paul set the church on a course that would lead it to spiritual peace.

Requires a New Attitude

"Rejoice in the Lord always. I will say it again: Rejoice" (v. 4).

Paul knew that it is impossible for Christians to harbor resentment and unforgiveness toward each other, and at the same time rejoice in the Lord Jesus. Therefore, his prescription for peace should not sound strange to us when, twice in one brief verse, he commanded the church to turn to praise.

This attitude of rejoicing that Paul commanded the Philippians to rediscover was not something strange to him. Although he was a Roman prisoner and his future was uncertain, he has more to say about joy and rejoicing in the Philippian Epistle than in any of his other writings. He had learned from experience that rejoicing in Jesus will put a song in the heart, a smile on the face, and a bounce in the step. And he knew that the Philippians desperately needed a new attitude if peace was to come again to their fellowship.

Requires a New Spirit

"Let your gentleness be evident to all" (v. 5). Euodia and Syntyche certainly had not been gentle with each other. If they had, the quarrel would never had come between them in the first place. So Paul commanded them, and all the Philippian believers, to forsake their partisan, quarrelsome spirit and cultivate a spirit of gentleness and kindness toward each other.

To the problem church at Corinth he writes the same thing:

Love is patient, love is kind. It does not envy, it does not boast, it is not proud. It is not rude, it is not self-seeking, it is not easily angered, it keeps no record of wrongs. Love does not delight in evil but rejoices with the truth. It always protects, always trusts, always hopes, always perseveres. Love never fails (1 Cor. 13:4-8).

When the gentleness of Jesus abounds in His followers, impatience is driven out, and patience replaces it. Anger is driven out, and kindness replaces it. Boastfulness is driven out, and humility replaces it. Self-centeredness is driven out, and concern for others replaces it.

Requires a New Sensitivity

"The Lord is near" (v. 5). Was Paul speaking of the second coming of Jesus, or he saying that Jesus is as near as our heartbeat and hears every unkind word that is spoken? Either way, it was a reminder to Euodia and Syntyche, and others who have been affected by their quarrel, that Jesus witnesses every unkind act and word.

Martin Luther recalled in later life that when he was a little boy he often looked at the stained-glass window in the parish church and would shrink at the sight of a frowning Jesus who was girded with a sword ready to lash out against the wicked.

Our Lord is not a frowning, vengeful Savior, but His heart is always grieved when the fellowship of His churches is divided. Paul told the Philippians that they should be done with their quarrelsome spirit, and remember that the sensitive Savior is a witness to everything said and done.

Requires a New Commitment

"Do not be anxious about anything, but in everything, by prayer and petition, with thanksgiving, present your requests to God" (v. 6).

This new commitment encouraged by Paul is one of complete dependence upon Jesus to supply all their needs. They cannot be quarreling among themselves and, at the same time, be fully depending upon Jesus. The two are incompatible.

Anxiety had replaced the peace of God that passed understanding in their fellowship. But that peace could be reclaimed through prayer, petition, and thanksgiving. Paul pointed out that one cannot truly pray with thanksgiving when one's attitude toward fellow believers is wrong. Thus, he called for a new commitment to fill their hearts that the old attitude might be pushed out.

They were to pray, with thanksgiving, and "Present your requests to God." The Greek could be literally translated: "Present your requests facing God." "Facing" God pictures fellowship with God. When a Christian is out of fellowship with God, his or her back, as it were, is toward God. When a believer is in fellowship with God, the Christian "faces" God. "Get your commitment to Jesus straightened out and then peace will return," he explained.

The Promise to the Church

"And the peace of God which transcends all understanding will guard your hearts and your minds in Christ Jesus" (v. 7).

This is not only a personal prescription for one who has a troubled heart, but it is also a corporate prescription for a church that has a troubled fellowship. When anxiety overwhelms the individual Christian, here is a blessed promise for him or her. And when problems overwhelm a church, here is a promise that is just as applicable for the church.

It Is a Dependable Promise

It is "the peace of God." It "will guard your hearts and your minds in Christ Jesus."

This is a powerful peace on which God Himself has a monopoly: it is "The peace of God." It is a quality of peace that cannot humanly be achieved or described: "[It] transcends all understanding." It is a dependable peace that will not only "guard your hearts" but also will guard "your minds." And it is a peace that is mediated only "in Christ Jesus" (v. 7).

It is a promise to a troubled church that God has a dependable peace for His church. All they have to do is accept it.

But one final thought needs to be added:

It Is a Conditional Promise

In the verses that follow, Paul told the Philippians that for peace to return to their troubled fellowship there were some conditions they must meet:

> Finally, brothers, whatever is true, whatever is noble, whatever is right, whatever is pure, whatever is lovely, whatever is admirable—if anything is excellent or praiseworthy—think about such things. Whatever you have learned or received or heard from me, or seen in me—put it into practice. And the peace of God will be with you (vv. 8-9).

There is the promise of peace Paul wrote, but don't overlook the conditions that must be met if the church is to have peace. Their minds that are filled with ignoble thoughts about each other must be filled with noble thoughts!

Conclusion

Have you ever read the legend about the land upon which the ancient temple was built? Herbert V. Prechnow tells the story in his book *Speaker's Source Book of Stories*.

Two brothers, according to the legend, had farms that joined on the very place where the temple was later built. One of the brothers was married and had a family, but the other was single. At harvest time one year, the married brother thought how lonely his single brother must be without a family to keep him company.

His life must be a lonely one, the married brother thought to himself. *I will take some of my sheaves from my harvest and add them to his harvest. Although I cannot give him a wife and children, I can make his life more pleasant by giving him some of the good things I have.*

The other brother thought to himself: *My married brother has a family to support and his harvest may not be sufficient to care for his family. I will share with him out of my abundant harvest.*

So at the time of harvest, one evening after the brothers returned from their fields to their respective homes, each gathered up an armload of sheaves, took them to the other's barn, and stacked the sheaves with those already there. In the morning, each brother looked at his larger stack of sheaves and wondered why they had increased during the night.

Then one night when the moon was full, the truth came out. The brothers happened to meet on the road, with full arms, going to the other's house to deposit his load of sheaves. And according to the legend, on that place where love was shown so beautifully, Solomon built his temple.

It's only a legend, of course, but there is a lesson in it. When members of a church love each other and express that love, peace and joy grow in that fellowship. And all are blessed.

Notes

1. Benjamin P. Browne, *Illustrations for Preaching* (Nashville: Broadman Press, 1977), 73.

2. Ibid, 74.

13
A Word for the Worrier

(Phil. 4:4-7)

Introduction

Worry is a problem common to all of us, but some handle it better than others. An unknown poet wrote about the worrier like this:

> He worried about the weather,
>   he worried about his health,
> He worried about his business,
>   he worried about his wealth.
> She worried about the children,
>   she worried about her clothes,
> She worried about the neighbors,
>   she worried about her woes.
>
> They worried about their taxes,
>   they worried about their pets,
> They worried about their future,
>   they worried about their debts.
> They worried, still they worried;
>   they worried, but alas,
> They worried about a lot of things,
>   that did not come to pass.

According to J. R. Grant who was president of Ouachita Baptist University in Arkadelphia, Arkansas, there is a way to worry scientifically. I don't know if the material was original with Dr. Grant, but

I am sure that in this scientific age if there is a way to worry scientifically, we need to know about it.

Dr. Grant gives twelve suggestions about how to worry scientifically:

1. Never worry over rumors or what "they" say.
2. Identify your worry problem by writing it down.
3. Worry only about one thing at a time.
4. Set a definite time for worry.
5. Never worry in bed, in the dining room, in living room, or at church.
6. When worry time comes, don't do it unless you can lean back in an easy chair in an air-conditioned room.
7. Set a time limit. If you go beyond the set time, give yourself credit for time-and-a-half worry.
8. Always smile, sing or whistle while you worry. Never frown while worrying.
9. Never worry when you are tired, sick, angry, hungry, or depressed.
10. Never worry while working, playing, visiting, shopping, or gossiping.
11. There are two times when you must refuse to worry: when you can help the situation, and when you can't help it.
12. Never worry alone. Take it to the Lord (Phil. 4:6).

It is this last suggestion that Paul addressed in this marvelous passage of Scripture. Writing to the Philippian believers, Paul had a word for the worrier.

The Problem

"Do not be anxious about anything" (v. 6). Here Paul identified the problem common both to the Philippian Christians and to believers today. He called it "anxiety." We call it "worry."

Paul recognized that even Christians worry. As incompatible with the Christian faith as that may be, the fact of the matter is: Christians worry.

About this problem of worrying that is common to all, Paul emphasized two things:

It Is a Present Problem

He wrote in verse 6: "Do not be anxious about anything." According to Kenneth Wuest, the word *anxious* means "worry, anxious care." It is a synonym for worry, Wuest said.

The grammatical construction of the words is strong. The literal translation reads, "quit habitually worrying!" Paul was not afraid they would begin to worry, they were already overwhelmed by it. He exhorted them to stop a thing already in progress.

Does this describe anyone you know? Is worry a present, daily problem to you? If it is, then Paul is addressing you: "Stop habitually worrying!"

It Is a Paralyzing Problem

Verse 4 indicates how worry paralyzes the worrier. Twice in this verse Paul told the Philippians, "Rejoice! Rejoice!" If they had already been rejoicing, to tell them to rejoice would have been unnecessary. They had fallen into Satan's trap. Worry had overtaken them. It trapped them, and joy was gone from life.

The paralyzing power of worry is further emphasized in verse 5: "Let your gentleness be evident to all." How gentle are they with each other? Why would Paul command gentleness if there were an abundance of it? It seems apparent that the quarrelsome spirit that had divided the church caused the joy bells to stop ringing in their hearts. They had become cross and irritable with each other. Pride had driven out humility. "The Lord is near. Be gentle with one another," Paul exhorted.

The Solution

Look at verse 6: "Do not be anxious about anything, but in everything, by prayer and petition, with thanksgiving, present your requests to God."

Nowhere in Scripture will one find a stronger and more comforting word for the worrier than this one. Paul gave us the steps, which, if followed, will lead us away from worry and by the still waters of inner peace. Notice the clear formula Paul listed to help the worrier.

We Are to Pray About What Worries Us

We are to pray "in everything." Everything that concerns us concerns our Heavenly Father. We are to share these concerns fully with him. Wuest wrote that the word here translated "prayer" speaks of prayer as an act of worship. Ralph Spaulding Cushman's words about this kind of prayerful worship are helpful:

> I met my God in the morning
> When my day was at its best,
> And His presence came like sunrise,
> Like a glory in my breast.
>
> All day long the Presence lingered,
> All day long He stayed with me,
> And we sailed in perfect calmness
> O'er a very troubled sea.
>
> Other ships were blown and battered,
> Other ships were sore distressed,
> But the winds that seemed to drive them
> Brought to us a peace and rest
>
> Then I thought of other mornings,
> With a keen remorse of mind,
> When I too had loosed the moorings,
> With the Presence left behind.
>
> So I think I know the secret
> Learned from many a troubled way:
> You must seek Him in the morning
> If you want Him through the day!

We Are to Talk to God About Our Personal Needs

The KJV translates "petition" (NIV) as "supplication." It means to pray about our personal needs. Some folks seem to think it's rather unchristian to pray about personal needs. *It's too selfish, too self-centered,* they reason. *We ought to pray for the church, the missionaries, the preacher, and everybody else in the world, but we should not be so concerned over our personal needs that we trouble the Heavenly Father with them,* some Christians seem to think.

Foolishness! Every personal concern we have concerns our Father. We are to take our personal needs to him.

We Are to Lay Our Requests Before God

"Requests" emphasizes the objects for which we would ask—"Namely, the things requested," as Wuest put it. It matters not how small or how large they are, we are to lay our requests at the feet of our Heavenly Father. We are to do it in faith, remembering that God's desire and ability to give are greater than our need, however great it may be. We are to do it, as a poet said it, remembering:

> Thou art coming to a king
> With thee great petitions bring,
> For his grace and power are such
> None can ever ask too much.

We Are to Pray with Thanksgiving

Read the Psalms and see how important thanksgiving and praise were to the psalmist. A thank-you note for a gift received is always a thoughtful and courteous thing to write. And to thank God for what He has given to us, even as we lay more requests before Him, is a thing in which He greatly delights.

How wise then we would be to follow the instructions of Psalm 100:

Enter his gates with thanksgiving and his courts with praise; give thanks to him and praise his name. For the Lord is good and his love endures forever; his faithfulness continues through all generations (Ps. 100:4-5).

Finally, we must follow Paul's instructions if we would experience:

The Results

What a great promise follows in verse 7: "And the peace of God, which transcends all understanding, will guard your hearts and your minds in Christ Jesus." The Holy Spirit is telling us here how to stay sane in an insane world! You see, Jesus is good for both the sweet by and by and the tough now and now! He will not only take me to heaven when I die, but He can also help me get through Monday!

There are two things about these results you must see.

They Are Heavenly Results

They come to us from the heart of God Himself: "And the peace of God"—it is peace which belongs to God and flows out from Him to us. He has a monopoly on it. It "transcends all understanding." Understanding this divine peace or explaining it to one who does not have it is impossible. It cannot be achieved or perceived by human intellect. It is God's faith gift to His obedient children.

They Are Powerful Results

This peace "will guard your hearts and your minds in Christ Jesus." "Will guard" could also be translated "shall garrison." It is a military term meaning "shall mount guard."

The Philippians could relate to this kind of picture. Being a Roman colony, they daily saw soldiers guarding the city. The soldiers kept out all that would concern or hurt the citizens.

As we meet the requirements stated in these verses, God's peace, like a well-armed soldier, shall mount guard over our heart and mind to keep us at peace in the midst of life's most pressing circumstances. What appropriate words these are for the worrier.

Conclusion

In his book *Stay Alive All Your Life*, Norman Vincent Peale wrote about George A. Straley, a sexton in a large church in a big city. Straley was puzzled by a crumpled piece of paper he found each week in the corner of one of the church's pews. Every week it was there, in the same place.

Smoothing out the crumpled piece of paper one day, Straley saw written on it several words: "Clara, ill; Lester, job; rent."

He began to watch the pew on Sunday mornings to see who was sitting in it. Soon he discovered it was a middle-aged woman. She was plain looking, but her countenance had a kind expression. She was an unassuming person who always came to church alone.

Straley took some of the notes to the pastor and told him about the woman who came every Sunday and sat in the same pew. The pastor read the words on the crumpled paper but didn't understand what they meant.

The next Sunday the pastor determined to meet the woman. As he greeted the worshipers at the door, the woman came by and the pastor asked her if she would wait for a few minutes and talk to him.

Showing her the notes, the pastor asked what they meant. Emotionally moved, the woman hesitated before she answered. Telling the pastor she knew he would think she was silly, she replied that on one of the city buses she rode regularly she had seen the sign, "Take your worries to church and leave them there."

"Pastor, I write my worries down every Sunday morning on those little pieces of blue paper. When the service is over, I leave them in the pew." she said. "I think God wants me to leave my problems at church."

On his way back to his study that Sunday noon, the pastor paused by the lady's pew, saw a piece of blue crumpled paper and picked it up: "John, in Korea," it read.

It's good advice to take our worries to church and leave them there. But we don't have to wait until Sunday morning to take our worries to the Heavenly Father. His door is always open.

14
Learning to Handle Life

(Phil. 4:10-19)

Introduction

In 1923 a group of America's most successful financiers met at the Edgewater Beach Hotel in Chicago. Walter Knight wrote in his book *Knight's Master Book of New Illustrations*, that among those present were Charles Schwab, the president of the largest independent steel company in America; Samuel Insull, the president of America's greatest utility company; Howard Hopson, the president of the largest gas company; and Richard Whitney, the president of the New York Stock Exchange.

Also present were Albert Fall, a member of the cabinet of the President of the United States; Jesse Livermore, the financier; Ivan Krueger, the head of the world's largest monopoly; and Leon Fraser, the president of the Bank for International Settlements.

By 1948, twenty-five years later, look what had happened to those men:

Charles Schwab, the president of the largest independent steel company, had lived on borrowed money for five years before his death and had died bankrupt. Samuel Insull, the president of the greatest utility company, had died penniless, a fugitive from justice. Howard Hopson, the president of the largest gas company, was dead. Richard Whitney, the president of the New York Stock Exchange, had only recently been released from Sing Sing Prison.

Albert Fall, the member of the President's cabinet, had been pardoned from prison so he could die at home. Jesse Livermore, the Wall Street financier, had died a suicide. Ivan Krueger, the head of the world's largest monopoly, had committed suicide. And Leon Fraser, the president of the Board for International Settlements, had also committed suicide.

There is a sobering lesson here: either we will handle life or life will handle us.

In this passage of Scripture, Paul wrote that he has learned the secret of how to handle life. He has been through it all—shipwrecks, hunger, cold, prison, prosperity, good times and bad times—and he told the Philippians he has learned the secret of handling life: "I have learned the secret of being content in any and every situation, whether well fed or hungry, whether living in plenty or in want" (v. 12).

We Must Not Be Ashamed to Lean on Others

Epaphroditus, a member of the Philippian church, had been sent by the church to check on Paul's condition. They knew he was a prisoner, so they sent Epaphroditus with some necessary things to make life a bit more comfortable for the imprisoned apostle.

In thanking them for their kindness, Paul wrote: "I rejoice greatly in the Lord that at last you have renewed your concern for me. Indeed, you have been concerned, but you have had no opportunity to show it" (v. 10).

In verse 14 he told them: "Yet it was good of you to share in my troubles." In verse 15, he confessed that on his missionary journeys they were the only church that was thoughtful enough to help supply his needs.

But he hastened in verse 17 to assure them that he didn't have his hand out—that he was no beggar—lest they misunderstand him. And in verse 18 he spoke about "the gifts you sent" and called them "A fragrant offering, an acceptable sacrifice, pleasing to God."

These expressions of helpfulness from a thoughtful church and Paul's response, show us that we Christians must lean on each other if we are going to handle life well. Everybody needs a friend and a helping hand sometime.

One of the greatest Christians of the early centuries was Tertullian. Born about A.D. 150 at Carthage in North Africa, he was the first theologian to use the word *trinitus*—Trinity—to describe the Godhead.

In his *Apology* Tertullian told how the early Christians helped each other, ministering to the sick, to those in need, or to those being persecuted. He wrote that "a love so noble" had made a great impression on those who were set against the Christians. Tertullian wrote that the enemies of Christ said of the Christians, "See how they love one another."

This is the kind of love the Philippians had for Paul and he for them. But love is more than a four-letter word. Love is alive and active and expresses itself as Paul so clearly wrote in 1 Corinthians 13.

Although we may not recognize it, we benefit from what others have done. When Eli Whitney invented the cotton gin, he put clothes on my back. When Alexander Graham Bell invented the telephone, he made communication possible for me. When Louis Pasteur perfected the process by which one can be immunized against disease, he protected me from smallpox, rabies, and other dreaded diseases. When the Curies discovered radium, they made radiation against cancer possible for me. When Gutenberg developed the printing press, he made books possible for me. And when Edison invented the electric light bulb, he turned night into day for me.

None of us is an island unto himself. It is kind and Christian to help those in need, as the Philippians helped Paul. But it is no less kind and Christian to accept help from others when we need it, as Paul did. It is certainly "more blessed to give than to receive," as Jesus told us (Acts 20:35). But it is blessed to do both!

So if we are going to learn to handle life, we must learn to lean on each other, and let others help us when we hurt.

We Must Accept What We Cannot Change

I am not saying this because I am in need, for I have learned to be content whatever the circumstances. I know what it is to be in need, and I know what it is to have plenty. I have learned the secret of being content in any and every situation, whether well fed or hungry, whether living in plenty or in want (vv. 11-12).

What mighty and moving words are these! Paul had "learned the secret of being content in any and every situation" (v. 12). What a marvelous thing it is to be able to accept what we cannot change. Surely this is one of the great principles of learning how to handle life.

Well did Reinhold Niebuhr express this attitude in his prayer:

God, Give us grace to accept with serenity the things that cannot be changed, courage to change the things which should be changed, and the wisdom to distinguish the one from the other.

Epaphroditus had brought to Paul some things he needed. Now, out of gratitude to these believers, Paul wrote them this thank-you letter. He reminded them that he did not depend upon their gifts, but he was grateful for them. He told them that he could get along without their love gifts, for his commitment was not based on things.

He had been in prison for sometime, and he said quite boldly that he had been neglected: "I rejoice greatly in the Lord that at last you have renewed your concern for me." But he gently excused their neglect: "You have been concerned, but you had no opportunity to show it" (v. 10). He then added: "I am not saying this because I am in need" (v. 11).

The word translated "need" describes Paul's condition. It is the same word used by Jesus in Mark 12:44 where He described the poor widow who put her two mites into the treasure: "They all gave out of their wealth; but she, out of her poverty, put in everything—all she had to live on." Paul's "need" and the widow's "poverty" are the same word.

This was Paul's condition when Epaphroditus arrived with the welcome gifts. Add to this the fact that Paul was chained to a Roman guard day and night, and we begin to understand his circumstances.

But what was his reaction to these stressful circumstances over which he had no control? Did he become angry and impatient with God? Did he complain? No, he left that type of behavior to others. His response is beautifully stated in verse 11: "I have learned to be content whatever the circumstances."

Explaining some of those circumstances, he added:

> I know what it is to be in need, and I know what it is to have plenty. I have learned the secret of being content in any and every situation, whether well fed or hungry, whether living in plenty or in want (v. 12).

Paul had learned this lesson from years of suffering: in jail and out of jail; in travels bad and dangerous; often hungry and cold; from persecutions by pagans and sometimes from his fellow Jews. "I have learned the secret of being content," he said.

"Content" means "sufficient for one's self, independent of external circumstances." But this is not the testimony of a braggart. It is the testimony of a believer whose joy, peace, and contentment do not depend on things external.

The tree that grows on the edge of the precipice, bent and twisted by high winds, makes the most beautiful furniture, we are told. By accepting what the tree cannot change, beauty and usefulness are developed in it.

And so it is with us. A lot of things that befall us we will never be able to change. Faith won't change them. Prayer won't change them. Time won't change them. There are hard and difficult things we would change if we could. But we can't, and we must bear them and let them develop within us the character of our Lord.

Finally, if we are going to learn how to handle life:

We Must Draw Upon the Strength of Jesus

Paul now stated his dependence upon Jesus that is so familiar: "I can do everything through him [Christ] who gives me strength" (v. 13). He then adds: "And my God will meet all your needs according to his glorious riches in Christ Jesus. To our God and Father be glory forever and ever. Amen" (vv. 19-20).

Do you remember the story of the man who had just died and was reviewing the footsteps he had taken in life? He observed that over the mountains and difficult places of life where he had walked there was only one set of footprints. But over the smooth and easy places there were two sets of footprints clearly visible.

Turning to Jesus, the man said: "There is something I don't understand. Why is it that over life's easy places You walked by my side? I know You did because there are two sets of footprints along those ways. But over the rough and difficult places it seems I have walked alone. See, there is only one set of footprints there."

"It is true that when your life was easy I walked at your side," replied the Savior. "But where the way was hard and difficult, I carried you. That is why there is only one set of footprints over those places."

Something like that had been Paul's experience. Often he had walked through life's difficult and dark places, and Jesus had always seen him through. He had come, therefore, to the settled conclusion that he could handle anything in life as long as Jesus was with him. Then, to assure the Philippians that this could also be their experience, Paul exclaimed with joy: "And my God will meet all your needs according to his glorious riches in Christ Jesus" (v. 19).

In his book *Song of Glory,* William J. Reynolds wrote that Horatio G. Spafford came to the time in life when he couldn't go on alone. And out of that dark experience he wrote one of our best-loved hymns.

Spafford and sorrow were not strangers. He lost his extensive real-estate holdings in the terrible Chicago fire of 1871. His fourteen-year-old son, who was his namesake, died of scarlet fever in 1880. Friends in the Presbyterian Church to which Spafford belonged misunderstood. Thinking that the family was being punished for its sins, the Spaffords were finally asked to leave the church.

But the greatest tragedy of Spafford's life occurred in 1873. He had planned a trip to Europe with his family, but last-minute business matters required Spafford to remain in Chicago. Intending to take another ship a few days later, he kissed his wife and four daughters, ages two through seven, put them on the *Ville du Havre* ocean liner and waved good-bye as they set sail.

In the middle of the Atlantic the *Ville du Havre* was struck by the English ship *Lochearn,* and in twelve minutes the *Ville du Havre* sank. Mrs. Spafford survived, but their four daughters were drowned.

As soon as possible after having received the tragic news, Spafford sailed to join his wife in England. In midocean, the ship's captain called Spafford to the bridge and told him that this was about the place where the *Ville du Havre* had gone down. For some time Spafford stood on the bridge, then he went below to his cabin and penned the poem that later became one of the best-loved hymns of Christendom:

> When peace, like a river, attendeth my way,
> When sorrows like sea billows roll;
> Whatever my lot, thou has taught me to say,
> It is well, it is well with my soul.

Spafford, like Paul, discovered the same grace and strength to handle life by drawing upon the inexhaustible resources of Christ Jesus. That same strength is available to us and as we draw upon it we will learn much better how to handle life.

Conclusion

Scottish novelist Robert Louis Stevenson told me about an experience his grandfather had once had as he sailed on the stormy sea. The vessel was caught by a terrible storm and was in danger of being swamped by the huge waves. When the danger was the greatest and the storm was the fiercest, Stevenson's grandfather carefully walked up on deck to see how bad things really were.

What he discovered brought to him immense comfort. There was the captain of the ship lashed with ropes to the wheel, holding the vessel off the rocks, and carefully steering it to safer waters. The captain looked up and smiled, and that smile completely reassured the frightened passenger. Going back to his cabin, he said to himself: "We shall come through; I saw the pilot smile!"

That's our assurance, too. We Christians will handle life well, both its joys and its crises, if we remember that the Captain is at the wheel, He has His hand upon us, and is smiling.